Words

The Real Woman's Guide to Hair

"Fabulous book! A must for any fashionista."
Indran Rajendram

"Fantastic and informative! Absolutely loved it!!"
Catherine Sosic

*"This is a very informative book!!
I love it and it is simple to read and easy to understand!!!
It is a 'must' to have it!!!"*
Natalie

*"Wow! So much good, reliable information in this book! I
now have a new hair bible, fantastic work ladies!"*
Rebecca

"Fabulous! Very Informative."
Giselle Courtney

*"I am not surprised how well put this most informative book
is. It's the perfect gift for my wife as it clearly and succinctly
gives professional pointers on how to make the most of what
God gave you. My wife is excited already and I feel like I
have done her such a good turn with the help of Penny and
Angela's expert advice."*
David Clements

*"Just downloaded the book, from what I have read so far
about hair colour info is really in-depth, can't wait to read
the other chapters thanks to Angela & her co author."*
Chris Nolan

The Real Woman's Guide to Hair

Simple Tips for Your Hair Style and Colour, Face and Body Shape

Penny Martin, Expert Hair Stylist

Angela Barbagallo, Personal Stylist

The Real Woman's Guide to Hair: Simple Tips for Your Hair Style and Colour, Face and Body Shape

by

Penny Martin, Expert Hair Stylist
and
Angela Barbagallo, Personal Stylist

Please visit Penny Martin: **www.pennymartinhair.com**
Please visit Angela Barbagallo: **www.styleangel.com**

This book is dedicated to the wonderful clients we have had the honour of serving, by doing what we love, over many years in the hair, beauty, and fashion industry.

To our kids Bethany, Liam (Penny), Yasmine and Valentino (Angela) for being awesome and putting up with us working weekends and nights! We love you to the moon and back!

Contents

Preface

There is no doubt that putting a book like this together is a project of passion, a labour of love, and the result of many years of Penny and Angela looking after their clients.

Penny is the hair and colour expert who has had her hair salon for many years, and she is also a senior Train the Trainer of future hairdressers.

Angela is a personal stylist, face shape, colour and body shape expert as well as the author of *8 Ways of Looking Fabulous, Taller and Slimmer by Dressing the Best for Your Body Shape*.

Penny and Angela know their stuff about how you can look great and they have the happy and loyal clients to show for it.

They must disclose that Penny is the only hairdresser to come near Angela's hair with a pair of scissors, bleach, or hair colour.

They met six years ago at a bridal trade fair where Angela's husband, Salvatore, got talking to Penny and was quick to make introductions. (thanks Salvatore!) Angela had just had a bad colour-highlight experience and Penny was quick to offer advice on how she would be able to fix it.

Needless to say, they have lots to share and talk about when they do get together and this book is the result of their partnership.

There is something so powerful about being happy with your hair—it frames your face, it lifts the colour on your face, and it is on display at all times.

Penny and Angela have put this book together with all the advice about hair styles, hair colour, and face shapes they share every day with their clients.

They anticipate that you may have a few "a-ha!" moments and possibly a few "oh no!" moments as they uncover the facts about hair and colour.

Penny and Angela are truly honoured that you're taking the time to read the fruits of their labour of love and passion.

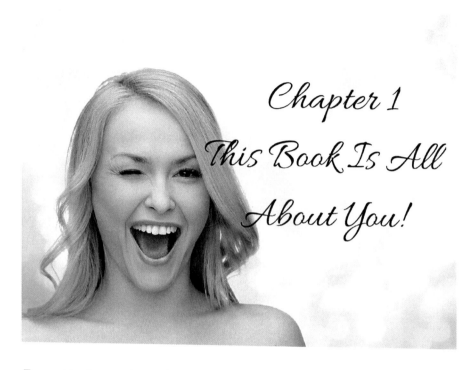

Chapter 1

This Book Is All About You!

From their combined fifty years of being in the "making you look and feel great" industry, Penny and Angela know what's troubling you when it comes to your hair.

Your concerns and questions are heard and understood. Reading this book will give you access to the experience of two hair and image professionals. This book is all about educating and empowering you so that your confidence will grow about your hair, your body, and what suits you.

The topics covered in this book are a reflection of what women, like you, have struggled with over the years.

It will help you to discover what your face shape is and, more importantly, what styles look great for your particular shape.

YOU are an individual and you have your preferred look, so Penny and Angela have put together a simple hair style personality quiz and corresponding styles that work really well for you.

There are many elements of you and your body that make up the perfect look that you feel comfortable in and all those areas are going to be addressed. Topics like your body shape, your neck length, and your profile will all be revealed.

Hair characteristics such as fine hair, hair loss, and greying hair are often sensitive areas for women (and men for that matter), and you will find practical options in this book.

The topic of hair colour will be covered—in its full *purple rinse* glory—from the basics of colour to how to fix your hair if your do-it-yourself home colour kit didn't work out, and you are now a gorgeous shade of orange or khaki green.

Hair colour is one juicy topic and Penny Martin is like a gorgeous scientist with a huge amount of skill and technique in this area, so they are excited for you to get to that section!

Keratin and other hair chemicals like silicone that you may be exposed to every day will be addressed so you can make an educated purchase in future.

This is a *real woman's guide to hair*! Enjoy!

Penny Martin's Passion for Your Hair

What Penny loves the most about what she does is that every time it is different. The clients are never the same twice, so it's a fresh start every time, with maybe a new look (sometimes the same look), and there is always a different conversation. It's kind of an evolving space.

Why do women travel for miles to see Penny? Simple, she cares about them, and she makes time to look after them and becomes immersed in their world, tuning in to their needs at that time.

Hair Stylist, Penny Martin

Why do they stay? The effort and energy Penny puts into all that she does shows in the happiness with their hair when they leave. They know that she really does care, that she is creative but constant.

Penny really does love all aspects of her career and puts great effort into all she does while, at the same time, keeping a project approach (start, middle, finish). She wants to know that she has done the best job she can.

Penny takes one day at a time, plans, and stocks up beforehand. No two days in her life are ever the same, and she loves that. It's an honour to work for a client and be trusted. Her self-motivation is huge. She knows she has created a business with her bare hands as an individual unit and she doesn't have to answer to a big company or a boss.

Even with her teaching career, Penny can do it her way within the learning elements. She thinks it's great to be creative and help to inspire others.

If Penny had to think about what legacy she would like to leave, it would be that she always did the best she could with one hundred percent effort! Every job has to be better than the last one. She is proud to have had a trusted position in image making and friendships.

What drives Penny? She makes every day count and never wastes a day being unproductive.

Angela Barbagallo's Passion for Your Confidence

In 2000, Angela made a decision that completely changed her life. She had no idea that starting a small personal shopping consultancy called Style Angel Corporation, which styled mostly corporate MEN (!) at the start, would turn into a Style Angel empire that helps WOMEN all around the Globe to be CONFIDENT in the way they look.

Personal Stylist,
Angela Barbagallo

CONFIDENCE translates into all areas of your life. When you're confident, you walk with a spring in your step, the glass is half-full, the kids behave, and there is a flow to life that is intoxicating.

When your hair is right, it simply feels awesome! All those hours looking like a citizen of planet Venus with a million-and-one foils on your head are worth it in the end.

In this book, Angela will share some simple tips to decide what hair styles will match your face shape so you are educated and armed the next time your hairdresser recommends a new fashion trend.

"Information is power" is the philosophy that both Penny and Angela share in how they look after their clients. They love sharing their knowledge so you feel stronger.

As a little girl, Angela grew up in the 70s where, for some reason, haircuts that resembled a plant pot were in fashion. If she was asked, "What do you want to be when you grow up?" her answer was always "a hairdresser." The thought of making women feel beautiful when they left her salon was so exciting for her.

Angela's journey in life took a few side turns and mixed with other passions. She now has a thriving personal styling business and she is lucky to be able to work with the Australian fashion label, Diana Ferrari, as their style consultant.

She is passionate about sharing her expertise of body shapes and what styles work and she has written a book available on Amazon called *8 Ways to Look Fabulous, Taller and Slimmer by Dressing the Best for Your Body Shape*.

So, here you have it. This book is a project of passion, and Penny and Angela both hope you enjoy the read as much as they have enjoyed writing it!

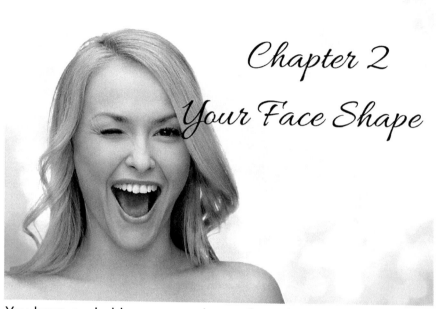

Chapter 2

Your Face Shape

You have probably compared your face shape to a celebrity's and could never really work out if your face shapes were the same.

When it comes to suitable hair styles, there are three things that, from a hair dressing and styling point of view, matter the most in terms of style and colour recommendation and these are:

1. Is your face shape significantly *longer than wider?*
2. Is your face shape really *round?*
3. Is your face shape really *angular?*

Here is how you can discover your own face shape. All you need is a mirror and a hard ruler.

Step 1:
Measure the length of your face from the base of your hairline to your chin.

Step 2:
Measure the width of your face across the widest part of your face from the left side of your face to the right side.

Step 3:
Is your face longer than it is wider? If so, you have a LONG face shape (scroll through to Style Recommendations).

Step 4:
Is your face almost as wide as it is long? Is your face full in the cheeks? If so, you have a ROUND face shape (scroll through to Style Recommendations).

Step 5:
Is your face shape really angular and sharp in the jaw line and chin? If so, you have an ANGULAR face shape (scroll through to Style Recommendations).

Discover Your Face Shape

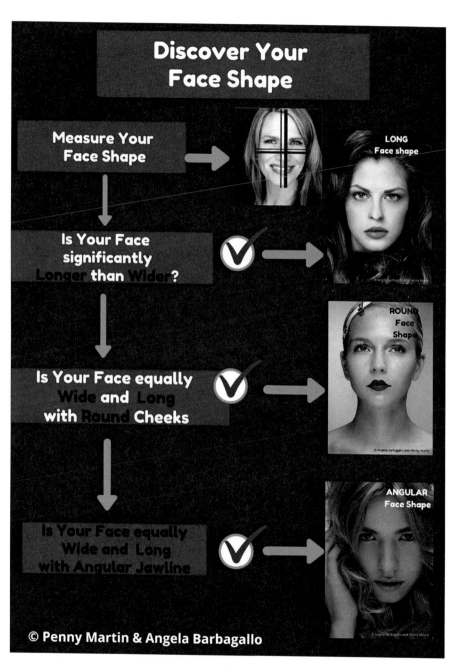

Measure Your Face Shape →

LONG Face shape

Is Your Face significantly Longer than Wider? ✓→

ROUND Face Shape

Is Your Face equally Wide and Long with Round Cheeks ✓→

ANGULAR Face Shape

Is Your Face equally Wide and Long with Angular Jawline ✓→

© Penny Martin & Angela Barbagallo

Long, Round, and Angular Face Shapes

LONG Face Shape Hair Styles

Your goal is to look for hair styles that visually shorten and/or add width to your face and soften your jaw line.

Great hair styles will tick some, if not all, of the points below

✓ Pick natural-looking styles.

✓ Choose styles that add width at your temples.

✓ Hair that has some height (but not too much) on top of your head and some width above your ears is good.

✓ A fringe is good if you have a high forehead. For smaller-depth foreheads, a straight and wispy or swept off to the side and not-too-thick fringe is best.

✓ The sides should be off your face, either swept back or short.

✓ Use off-centre or side parts.

✓ Hair length should be medium to medium short.

✓ Long hair must have plenty of width at the neckline.

✓ Widening hair styles, such as soft curls or a long bob, really suit a long face shape.

✓ Use a lot of highlights so attention goes to the different shadings in your hair instead of your longer face.

Preferably, you should use three colour highlights: one 3 shades lighter than your original colour, one 1 shade lighter, and one 1 shade darker than your original hair colour.

Hair Styles to Avoid

✓ Highly stylized styles, e.g., angular cuts, severely slicked down hair, extremely short hair, etc.

✓ Height only on top of your head.

✓ Long, straight hair.

✓ Hair close to the sides of your head.

✓ Centre parts.

✓ Hair combed straight back if you have a high forehead.

Short Hair Styles for a LONG Face Shape

The Right Short Hair Style - Create Width
The heavy top layers fall into a rounder shape while the fringe almost halves the vertical length making the face and chin appear shorter and more balanced. This same shape will work on any other hair texture.

Right and Wrong SHORT Hair Styles for a LONG Face Shape

© Penny Martin and Angela Barbagallo

The Wrong Short Hair Style for a Long Face Shape - Avoid Height

The worst thing that you can do is to make your face appear even longer, as is the case with this hairstyle.

Medium Hair Styles for a LONG Face Shape

The Right Medium Hair Style - Create Width

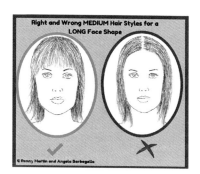

This is a soft wavy hair style with body that really suits your oblong LONG face shape. The fringe helps to shorten the overall length of the face while the layers help add body and bounce creating needed width. This shape will work with straight or curly hair.

The Wrong Medium Hair Style for a LONG Face Shape
The middle part creates more vertical length while the flimsy sides do nothing to build width. This hair style lacks body and needs to be shortened in shape (not length).

Long Hair Styles for a LONG Face Shape

The Right Long Hair Style - Create Width
This is a soft, wavy hair style with body that really balances your LONG face shape. The fringe helps to shorten the overall

length of the face while the layers near your face help add body and bounce creating needed width. This shape will work with straight or curly hair.

Right and Wrong LONG Hair Styles for a LONG Face Shape

© Penny Martin and Angela Darbegallo

The Wrong Long Hair Style for a LONG Face Shape
Having a part in the middle of your head that divides your hair in two longer portions will give your face an even longer look. The dead straight long length will add even more length to your face.

ROUND Face Shape Hair Styles

A round face is one that looks almost as long as it is wide and has full cheeks. Your goal is to choose styles that visually *lengthen* your face.

Great hair styles will tick some, if not all, of the points below:

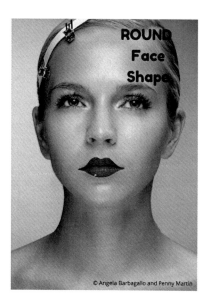

ROUND Face Shape

© Angela Barbagallo and Penny Martin

✓ Choose styles that add a little bit of height to the top of your head and temples to balance the width of your cheeks.

✓ You can use colour to balance your face shape by going darker underneath on the bottom part of the head and lighter on the top layer.

✓ A good hair length is medium to long length with some tapering at the back.

✓ Keep your hair off your face and close in at the sides to show your cheekbones.

✓ A diagonal fringe is a great way to add length and interest to a round face.

Hair Styles to Avoid

✓ "Roundish" hair styles.

✓ Straight fringes, especially those that are heavy.

✓ Fullness at the ear line.

✓ Very short hair that follows the roundness of the face.

Short Hair Styles for a ROUND Face Shape

The Right Short Hair Style - Create Height

This hairstyle adds height and makes your round face appear longer than it actually is. You need to focus on adding height not width, which is exactly what this hairstyle does.

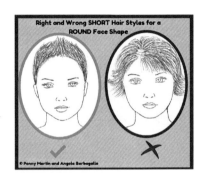

The Wrong Short Hair Style for a ROUND Face Shape
This hair style adds width and makes your round face appear wider than it already is. The fringe makes your face shorter while the sides that kick out make your face wider.

Medium Hair Styles for a ROUND Face Shape

The Right Medium Hair Style - Create Height

This hair style gives the appearance of an oval shape. The sides pulled back behind the ears help slim the face down, while no fringe shows off your forehead and therefore a longer shape. The off-centre part helps divide

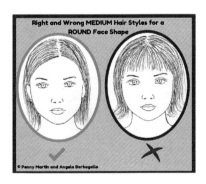

the face evenly making it also appear longer rather than wider.

The Wrong Medium Hair Style for a ROUND Face Shape
This example shows how adding width rather than length to a round face shape is disastrous. The fringe shortens the face while the hair that kicks out at chin length only accentuates width and roundness.

Long Hair Styles for a ROUND Face Shape

The Right Long Hair Style - Create Height
The middle part helps divide your face into two longer portions while the absence of bangs doesn't compromise any vertical length. If your hair is straight it would create even more slimness in your face.

The Wrong Long Hair Style for a ROUND Face Shape Although having volume at the crown can sometimes be a good thing, this style adds width to the sides, which makes your face appear wider and incredibly round. The fringe will cover your face up too much.

ANGULAR Face Shape Hair Styles

An angular face is one that looks almost as long as it is wide; has full cheeks; and a broad, shallow jawline. It is also a face shape that could become round with weight gain. Your goal is to look for hair styles that visually *lengthen* your face and *soften* your jaw line (if desired).

© Angela Barbagallo and Penny Martin

Great hair styles will tick some, if not all, of the points below

✓ Add volume to your hair in the area of the eyes and the top of the crown away from your jaw line.

✓ Create the illusion of height to offset the angular shape with unbalanced lines—curve and angle hair across the forehead.

✓ Natural looking soft styles are essential to soften your angular face shape.

✓ Choose styles with broken or asymmetric lines.

✓ Use foils to soften your chin area, feminize it up by creating a sun-kissed look, or perhaps balayage (a freehand technique where the hair colour is applied by hand in a sweeping motion).

✓ Hair longer than the ears should be kept close to the face.

✓ Styles longer than your chin should have curves to soften your jaw line.

✓ Avoid showing too much or too little forehead.

✓ Use an off-centre part with a swept-to-the-side fringe.

✓ Keep your hair close at the ears to emphasize your cheekbones.

✓ Cut your hair a bit longer at the back to lengthen the face.

Hair Styles to Avoid

✓ Too much fullness at the ears.

✓ Straight fringes, especially those that are heavy.

✓ Centre parts (makes jaw look angular).

Short Hair Styles for an ANGULAR Face Shape

The Right Short Hair Style - Create Height and Softness
This hair style adds height and makes your angular face appear longer than it actually is. You need to focus on adding height not width, which is exactly what this hair style does.

The Wrong Short Hair Style for an ANGULAR Face Shape This hair style adds height and makes your angular face appear wider than it already is. The fringe makes your face shorter while the sides that kick out makes your face wider.

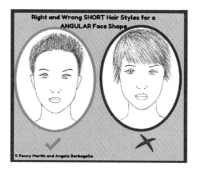

29

Medium Hair Styles for an ANGULAR Face Shape

The Right Medium Hair Style - Create Height and Softness

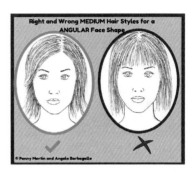

This short concave bob is a great-looking hair style for your angular face shape. The sides falling forward soften the jaw line, while the diagonal bangs are also ideal for minimizing strong angles. The hair style has an overall rounded appearance making it the right choice for framing angular face shapes. Other short styles that will work for your face shape include looks that have soft, wispy, side-parted swept-across bangs in wavy or curly textures.

The Wrong Medium Hair Style for an ANGULAR Face Shape
This hair cut illustrates really well what to avoid on angular face shapes. Firstly, the top area, although wispy, has a very square shape about it. Secondly, the short tapered sides accentuate the angles coming up from the jaw line, and the square hairline only adds to what is doomed from the very start.

Long Hair Styles for an ANGULAR Face Shape

The Right Long Hair Style - Create Height and Softness

This hair style has all the right ingredients to suit and compliment your angular face. Firstly, the sides are soft and wispy falling onto the jaw line hiding squareness. Secondly, a side part and side-swept bangs help create a diagonal illusion or deception that loses any focus on angles. The graduated sides and back angle upwards creating a

whole new shape to frame your face. Other variations in different textures and slight length adjustments will also work keeping to this theme.

The Wrong Long Hair Style for an ANGULAR Face Shape

This hair style looks very heavy and solid all over making it a bad choice for square face shapes. The heavy bangs create a very square shape by themselves, but once they are added to the straight one-length sides and back, the result is very square and angular. The sides need layers, particularly around the face, while the bangs need to be less heavy and more diagonal.

Chapter 3
Your Body
Shape and
Characteristics

There are a few areas in this chapter that are very important elements of YOU, and they will help you to decide which hair styles, accessories, and clothes look fantastic on you.

You may not have given much thought to your neck length and width, or your size and body height, or the fact that you have a large or small nose, but in this chapter you will be taken behind the scenes of how hair and style minds work during your appointment.

Information is everything and there is no need to impress your hairdresser with lingo, but an awareness of your own body and hair will make it easier for the hairdresser in charge of your hair, if they know what they're doing.

You may have sat in a salon chair praying to the heavens above to "Please, let me have a good outcome." How many times have you been utterly disappointed, gone back to get your hair fixed and sat through the ordeal with knots in your stomach?

Your hair is such an incredible feature and one wrong turn, one do-it-yourself colour kit, or one sneaky salon coupon at-50% off-from-groupon.com-that-is-such-a-fantastic-bargain can turn it bad.

Gosh, this fact in itself is the conception of how this passion project came together—Angela came to Penny because of an incompetent hairdresser who put some hideous coloured foils on Angela's hair and the result was disastrous.

The damage was done—damage that would be on show for everyone to see for many weeks—damage that could well take six to nine months to repair itself under the supervision of a hairdresser who knows what she is doing.

It sounds dramatic but, gorgeous woman, most likely what you care about the most is that you're happy with the result of your precious time and money spent in a hair salon. You want to be happy, listened to, and thrilled with the results.

Your Neck Area

Identifying your neck length and neck width is one of the first areas that gets ticked off in considering what hair styles, necklines, accessories, and glasses will suit you.

It is often an area that is not paid attention to, so you will be a winner once you have identified whether you have an extra long neck, or an extra wide neck, or an extra short neck.

It is the "extra" that should make your ears prick up as it may need balancing when it comes to your best hair style or necklace size. Your neck size will also come into account when you want to know if scarves will look good on you.

IS YOUR NECK?	LONG	MEDIUM	SHORT
WIDE	long and wide	medium and wide	short and wide
NORMAL	long and normal	medium and normal	short and normal
SLIM	long and slim	medium and slim	short and slim

Where do you sit in the scale above? Tick the box that describes your neck.

You can measure the length of your own neck, and learn the secret of how a stylist would measure your neck.

Make sure you have a ruler and you are wearing a necklace.

Have the top of your ruler next to the base of your ear lobe and hold it vertically to where your necklace sits on your shoulder. This is your neck length.

Your neck width is measured at the widest part of your neck.

Medium Length and Normal Width

Long Neck and Normal Width

The next few pages are filled with tips from a clothing and hair back ground when it comes to your neck.

Simply find your neck length and width category and discover what is best for your proportions.

IS YOUR NECK?	LONG (over 9 cm)	MEDIUM (between 6 and 9 cm)	SHORT (less than 6 cm)
WIDE	Medium-long to long hair is great. Short hair with flipped-back hair at neckline could work. 3 cm above to shoulder length hair suits best. Medium to large width of scarves. Medium to large pendant in the magic spot (see chapter below for details). Choose tops that are not too low like mid V-neck, cross over or round tops.	Medium-long to long hair is great. Short hair with flipped-back hair at neckline. Medium width of scarves are great so you don't cut off your neck. Medium to large pendant in the magic spot (see chapter below for detail). All necklines that work for your body shape will work for you.	A bob just under the ear looks great. Medium length hair looks best. Only use scarves that are medium in slimness and really practice how to tie in a V-neck to elongate neck. Medium pendant in the magic spot (see chapter below for details). Necklines that have a bit of depth are great to elongate your neck.

IS YOUR NECK?	LONG (over 9 cm)	MEDIUM (between 6 and 9 cm)	SHORT (less than 6 cm)
NORMAL	Medium-long to long hair is great. Short hair that has some width looks great. 3 cm above to shoulder length hair suits best. Medium to large width of scarves. Medium to large pendant in the magic spot (see chapter below for details). Choose tops that are not too low like mid V-neck, cross over, or round tops. Use a camisole to balance extra low-cut tops or dresses.	All hair styles and lengths that suit your overall height work for you. Medium width of scarves. Medium pendant or necklace in the magic spot (see chapter below for details). All necklines and top styles that suit your body shape work for you.	All elongating hair styles and lengths that suit your overall height work for you. Only use scarves that are medium in slimness and really practice how to tie in a V-neck to elongate neck. Medium pendant in the magic spot (see chapter below for details). Necklines that have a bit of depth are great to elongate your neck.

IS YOUR NECK?	LONG (over 9 cm)	MEDIUM (between 6 and 9 cm)	SHORT (less than 6 cm)
SLIM	Medium long hair with some width looks great. Medium to large width of scarves. 3 cm above to shoulder length hair suits best. Medium pendant in the magic spot (see chapter below for details). Choose tops that are not too low like mid V-neck, cross over, or round-neck tops. Use a camisole to balance extra low-cut tops or dresses.	All hair styles and lengths with extra width that suit your overall height work for you. Medium width of scarves. Medium pendant or necklace in the magic spot (see chapter below for details). All necklines and top styles that suit your body shape work for you.	All hair styles and lengths with extra width that suit your overall height work for you. Only use scarves that are medium in slimness. Medium to small pendant in the magic spot (see chapter below for details). Round neck, cowl, and soft scoop necklines work for you.

A Friendly Posture Reminder

Have you ever checked to see how much your shoulders slope and if indeed one side slopes more than the other? Have you perhaps carried a heavy handbag on one shoulder for too many years, or carried a few babies on one side, or have sat in a certain incorrect posture over the keyboard in your office for many years.

You may need to see a physiotherapist or other posture specialist so you are *tuning* your body like a well maintained car. Often, it is your core strength that needs work to support your body and hold you in position.

So, for the rest of this book, if you could pull your belly button in to your back, pull your shoulders back, and put your chest forward that would be great!

Of course just kidding, but please take good care of your body and posture!

Harmony of Scale

When it comes to jewellery choices, there are no firm rules of right or wrong. However, just as you consider your size and build when choosing items of clothing, you should consider the same things when choosing accessories. The aim is always to have you wearing the accessory, not the accessory wearing you.

Height, Weight, and Bone Structure

Your wrist and ankle circumference determines your bone structure. The combination of your weight, height, and bone structure determines your scale.
Make sure you match your scale with your choice of size of accessories to look harmonious at all times.

	Height, Weight, and Bone Structure		
	LARGE	**MEDIUM**	**SMALL**
Jewellery size	Large to medium	Medium	Small to medium
Scarf size	Large width tied in V-neck	Medium	Small
Neckline	V-neck, cross over, scooped, deep round	Medium width V-neck, cross over, scooped, round, and boat neck	Small width V-neck, cross over, scooped, round
Pattern size	Large to Medium	Medium to small	Small to medium
Hair	Medium length and width	Any length and width	Short to medium length and width

The Ideal Spot for Your Necklace

The placement of a pendant or necklace is measured differently for every neckline of your dress or top. Place one finger at the base of your neck and one finger at the top of your neckline. Divide this area in half and there you have found the magic spot where a pendant will look amazing!

You may choose to wear a multiple layered necklace and for the best balanced look make sure the middle layer of your necklace is in the ideal spot.

How to Tie a Scarf and Look Slimmer Instantly

To make it easy, your personal stylist, Angela, has made a step-by-step video on her Pinterest TV channel. Just log in to Pinterest and search for styleangel3 and you will find a number of videos that show you how to choose the best scarf size, pattern including a step-by-step guide on how to tie a scarf and look slimmer instantly videos you need.

Your Body Shape

When you know your body shape, it will give you clarity and you might say a few "Oh, that's why ..." but the most important thing is to focus on what styles work for your shape.

You can take the ideal styles for your shape and compare them to what you currently have in your wardrobe.

You will need a tape measure and a pen to write down your measurements. If you don't have a tape measure, simply cut a piece of string long enough to measure around your hips and grab a ruler.

Angela has prepared a diagram where you can simply follow the steps and work out what your body shape is.
To make the information relevant for you, she has prepared lots of information on the Style Angel website, Pinterest, and YouTube, which you can access just by clicking on your body shape image.

Just follow the prompts below.

How to Measure Your Body Shape

Each shape has amazing style options and Angela is going to show you how you can work your body shape to your best advantage with simple steps, and she means any weight from size 6 to 26+!

STEP 1 - YOUR BUST: With a tape measure, measure yourself from your back around the fullest part of your bust (over the nipple line) with your bra on. Write down this measurement.

STEP 2 - YOUR WAIST: Hold your legs still and move your upper body. Put your index finger on the pivoting point in your waist where your upper body pivots on your lower body.

Welcome to your waist!! Measure around your waist with the tape measure. Write down this measurement.

STEP 3 - YOUR HIPS: With a tape measure, measure yourself around the fullest part of your bottom. Write down this measurement.

Follow the simple questions below in the body-shape chart.

BODY SHAPE **CALCULATOR**

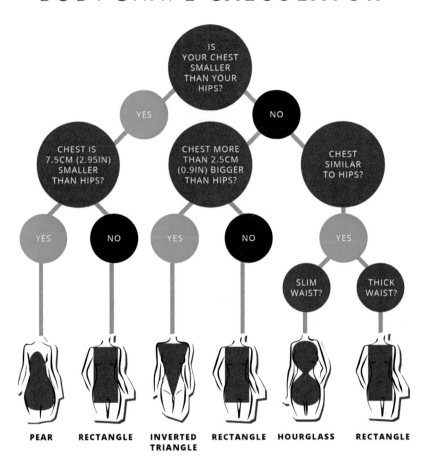

IS YOUR CHEST SMALLER THAN YOUR HIPS?

YES — **CHEST IS 7.5CM (2.95IN) SMALLER THAN HIPS?**

YES — **PEAR**

NO — **RECTANGLE**

NO — **CHEST MORE THAN 2.5CM (0.9IN) BIGGER THAN HIPS?**

YES — **INVERTED TRIANGLE**

NO — **RECTANGLE**

NO — **CHEST SIMILAR TO HIPS?**

YES — SLIM WAIST? — **HOURGLASS**

THICK WAIST? — **RECTANGLE**

APPLE

NOTE: If you fall in the Rectangle Body Shape category and your waist measurement is larger than hips and bust. Your shape is **Apple.**

style angel ©
giving you confidence in the way you look

Style Angel Corp Pty Ltd ©

How to Dress for Your Body Shape

Congratulations, you are now in the elite group of women who know their body shape.

It is very likely you rolled your eyes as you discovered your shape. Angela wanted to mention this as she sees this all the time when she measures clients in person. Angela never hears a big cheer, it is more like a "Yes that makes sense".

Research shows that 91% of women are not happy with their body shape so rest assured there is no right or wrong body shape! Every body shape has its great parts and its challenges. You are well and truly on your way to learn everything you need to know to make great choices for your shape.

Now that you know what your body shape is, you're probably excited to find out how you can dress for your shape! You will find dedicated chapters for each body shape all with do's and don'ts and special areas to focus on.

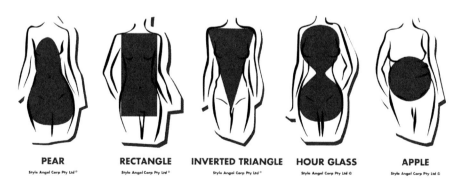

PEAR   RECTANGLE   INVERTED TRIANGLE   HOUR GLASS   APPLE

Style Angel Corp Pty Ltd ©   Style Angel Corp Pty Ltd ©   Style Angel Corp Pty Ltd ©   Style Angel Corp Pty Ltd ©   Style Angel Corp Pty Ltd ©

PEAR Body Shape

Your PEAR shape is the body shape category that the majority of women fall into. The good thing about that is that lots of big retailers know that this is where the money is so they design more styles that suit PEAR shaped shoppers.

PEAR

As two PEAR shaped ladies, Penny and Angela know the issues that are running through your head right now. Finding pants is a nightmare, finding skirts to fit your waist is hard, if a dress fits in the bottom it is too big in the top, jeans often fall off your bottom when you bend over and short skirts are a big no-no. On the flip side, tops are fairly easy to find, buttons on shirts don't usually pop and your waist is your biggest asset! Have we hit the nail on the head?

Your aim is to visually broaden your upper body to balance out your lower body.

DO'S
✓ Use Horizontal lines upper body.
✓ Bring the attention upwards to the bust area, puff sleeves broaden the shoulders to balance your lower body.
✓ Dresses that are body-hugging on the top, accentuate your tiny waist and then drape outwards, drawing a

discreet veil over the width of your thighs. (wrap dresses are a great style to try).

✓ Big lapel jackets and wide-cut necklines serve to broaden the appearance of your shoulders, balancing the bottom half.

✓ A cropped jacket gives the illusion of lengthening your legs and it's sufficiently hugging to enhance your well defined waist.

✓ Broad lapels on a winter jacket draw the eye to your shoulders and show a shapely torso. Make sure the coat flares to the knee, covering the bulge of your thighs.

✓ A jumper worn over a shirt, t-shirt or blouse moulds to your figure and gives you a curvy shape.

✓ Wide-leg or straight pants in a flat fronted style that hang from the top of your bottom and don't cling to your thighs.

✓ Wear a darker colour on the lower half of your body to help slim the legs.

✓ Use vertical lines lower body.

✓ Straight and slightly flared skirts (A-line is a good choice).

✓ Shape wear that is like biker pants to skim the thighs and bottom and enhance the slim waist and flat stomach.

DON'TS

✓ Stiff fabrics.

✓ Shapeless garments.

✓ Side pockets on pants (look out for angled pockets that don't pull when you walk or appear to be straining).

✓ Full skirts with open pleats.

✓ Pencil skirts.

✓ Tapered pants (like the fashionable skinny jeans).

✓ Jodhpurs (like horse-riding pants).

✓   Spaghetti-strap tops.
✓   Jackets that cut across the bum.
✓   Stretched trousers of any kind.
✓   Ankle straps or stilettos.

Make sure you follow Style Angel on Pinterest as Angela will continue to add suitable styles that are currently online or in store.

RECTANGLE Body Shape

Your RECTANGLE shape is the body shape category that approximately 30% of women fall into. Usually as soon as Angela mentions that runway fashion models usually are RECTANGLE body shapes the client perks up.

As a body shape expert, Angela knows that is one of the easier body shapes to dress for as your body usually fills out the outfits out in all areas.

RECTANGLE

There is not so much to balance out, there are no huge hips and tiny top. The issues that you struggle with all the time that are running through your head right now could be; "I have no waist", "I am quite broad in the shoulders compared to most women", "I have large calves and boots are so tricky to fit me", "I feel my shape is so masculine even though I have big boobs".

On the flip side, tailored dresses are fairly easy to fit, pants are easy to fit in the thighs (but need to fit you around the tummy without showing a muffin top),and straight skirts look amazing on you.

A RECTANGLE woman will often appear shorter and heavier than she really is.
Many women find they become rectangular with age. The thickening of the mid-torso is most commonly a result of the vertebrae compressing and creating less torso length and less space to distribute any fat.

Your aim is to add definition to your shape by visually elongating the body and defining the shoulders (if you are overweight) or defining the waist (if you are slender).

DO'S
✓   Slight shaping of garments.
✓   A classic round-neck jumper gives elegant shape.
✓   Angular jackets that point to your waist.
✓   Shoulder-line emphasis.
✓   Dresses that wrap or flow through the waistline, feminine chiffon softens your shape.
✓   High waisted dresses (like a wrap dress) will add definition to your shape.
✓   Jackets that fasten with a tie belt or sash to create a waist.
✓   A three-quarter length coat that is belted (like a trench-coat), make sure you tie the jacket either at the front or the back. Hip pockets on the jacket add a bit of curve.

- ✓ A coat that is cut in an empire line that comes in at the waist.
- ✓ Straight and semi-fitted jackets and dresses.
- ✓ Straight to slightly flared flat fronted pants.
- ✓ High placed focal points.
- ✓ The gentle flare of an A-line skirts is all you need to add shape to your waist.
- ✓ Slightly flared pants that add shape to your waist.
- ✓ Accessories that focus the attention to the centre and the top part of your body.
- ✓ Fitted vest with a shirt, blouse or t-shirt underneath to carve into the body.
- ✓ Shape wear that shapes the waist.

DON'TS
- ✓ Clingy fabrics that accentuate the rectangle shape.
- ✓ Fitted silhouettes that accentuate the rectangle shape.
- ✓ Baggy pants.
- ✓ Big loose tops.
- ✓ Narrow skirts.
- ✓ Cropped tops.
- ✓ Dropped waist.
- ✓ Formless three-quarter length jackets.
- ✓ Boxy jackets.
- ✓ Double breasted coats.
- ✓ Mini-skirts.
- ✓ Trousers in a stiff fabric.

INVERTED TRIANGLE Body Shape

Your INVERTED TRIANGLE shape is the body shape category that less than 5% of women fall into.

Angela calls your shape a cocktail glass as you start broad and you narrow down in the legs.

The issues that you struggle with all the time that are running through your head right now could be; "I have no waist", "I am really broad in the shoulders compared to most women", "I have huge boobs and no where to hide them".

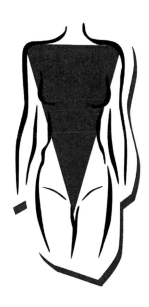

INVERTED TRIANGLE

Tops are a nightmare to find, button up shirts...pfff forget it. On the flip side; you have GREAT legs, tiny calves, pants are super easy to buy, straight skirts look amazing but you always need a small size and the waist can be a bit tight.

The aim is to create balance with the upper and lower body by creating the impression of a wider bottom and drawing attention away from the upper body.

DO'S

✓ Use horizontal lines lower body.
✓ Use vertical lines upper body.
✓ A draping dress that curves in all the right places (jersey accentuates your shape).
✓ Dresses that flow through the waist.
✓ A fluting skirt with a flaring hemline to balance top and lower half.
✓ A draping skirt that gathers on the hips (jersey is great).
✓ A-line skirts.
✓ A coat with buttons that sit underneath the bust.
✓ Set in sleeves.
✓ Side shaped garments.
✓ Good fitting bras.
✓ Shape wear that shapes from the bust and finishes at the bottom.
✓ Flared pants.

DON'TS

✓ Stiff fabrics.
✓ Emphasizing waist.
✓ Full sleeves.
✓ Big Collar.
✓ Tapered pants.
✓ Chunky knit sweaters.
✓ Double breasted jackets.
✓ Shift dresses.
✓ Polo necks.
✓ High waisted trousers.
✓ Bolero jackets.
✓ Elaborate necklaces.
✓ Shapeless floatie dresses.

✓ Three quarter sleeves or sleeves that finish at the bust line.
✓ Cut away shoulders.
✓ Scooped necklines.
✓ Shoulder pads.

HOURGLASS Body Shape

Your HOURGLASS shape is the body shape category that less than 5% of women fall into.

Your key is to always accentuate your waist and find tops and bottoms to not only show off your curves but that actually fit.

Clothes that are made generously in the bottom will leave a huge gap in your waist and alteration for you is almost always the only way.

Bra fittings can be difficult for you too as your cup size on average is DD+ and your band size small.

You have perfect proportions between your upper and lower body with a well defined waist. Dressing is often quite easy as many styles suit an

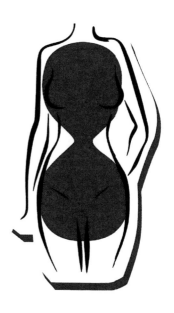

HOUR GLASS

hourglass shape. Your only limitations will come from other factors such as weight, prominent features, age, your shoulder-line etc.

Weight gain does not become apparent until you are moderately overweight, as the weight tends to be distributed evenly and the waist remains proportionally small.

DO'S
✓ Shapely garments especially at the waist
✓ Soft fabrics
✓ Emphasise curves without cluttering
✓ Straight and slightly flared pants and skirts (pencil skirts exaggerate the curve from the hip to the knee)
✓ Dresses that emphasise the waist
✓ Tops that fit the waist are wide open on the neckline and have something to divert the eye towards the shoulders like puffed sleeves.
✓ Simple jewellery.
✓ Jacket with curved lapel to show off curves, three quarter sleeves show off elegant wrists and suggest a delicate frame.
✓ Shirts that have side fastening (do not button all the way to the top)
✓ Cute shoes with rounded toes, peep toes or bows.
✓ Make sure that dress or top fits the bust foremost as it is easier to take things in at the back.
✓ A coat with a deep V and full skirt and pockets on the hips.

DON'TS
✓ Stiff fabrics.
✓ Cluttering the body.

✓ Baggy styles.
✓ Skirts with open pleats.
✓ Tapered pants.
✓ Flap side pockets on trousers.
✓ Big belts.
✓ Batwing sleeves.
✓ Deep V-neck fitted cardigans.
✓ Ankle strap shoes, pointy shoes like stilettos or cowboy boots.
✓ Watch that sleeves around the arms don't cut in.

APPLE Body Shape

Your APPLE shape is the body shape category that about 1% of women fall into. Even though most women THINK they are an APPLE shape when you do the measurements you should only be reading this information if you can say yes to all the following questions:

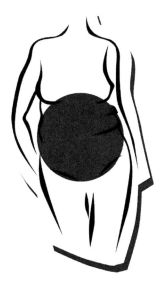

1. Your waist measurement is LARGER than your bust.
2. Your waist measurement is LARGER than your hips.
3. You weight classifies in the Obese or Very Overweight category.

APPLE

No doubt you are feeling

overwhelmed as your health could be in danger and finding items to wear is not easy. Mainstream stores don't stock your sizes and when you shop in Plus Size stores they don't always get the right styles right to make you look slimmer.

DO'S
✓   Semi-fitted, boxy and soft silhouettes.
✓   Low necklines.
✓   Tops and blouses worn out.
✓   T-shirts that are rushed in the middle (make sure they are long enough).
✓   A wide V-neck breaks up the size of your chest.
✓   A straight duster coat worn against contrasting colours and fabrics will break your body up into three long slim slices. Make sure the jacket finishes above the knee if you are short.
✓   Vertical design influence from the top to bottom.
✓   Well fitting bras.
✓   Support garments for your torso.
✓   Flat front straight and soft pants.
✓   Straight and subtly flared skirts.
✓   Loose fitting garments.
✓   Dresses that flow through the waistline.
✓   High placed focal points.

DON'TS
✓   High necklines.
✓   Over embellishments.
✓   Pleats.
✓   Waist emphasis.
✓   Belts.
✓   Tucking tops in.
✓   Large lapels.

- ✓ Full sleeves.
- ✓ Tight t-shirts.
- ✓ High waisted pants.
- ✓ Pleated waists.
- ✓ Puffer jackets.
- ✓ Men's jackets.

Will Your Body Shape Change?

You may ask yourself, will my body shape change? YES, there is a possibility, and here is why: When you have had children and/or you are going through Menopause you will find that your waist thickens a lot, your stomach is not as flat and female curves may appear on your back (also called back fat but we think female curves sounds much nicer!).

You might also increase in cup size and even the band size.

You may not know that when going through Menopause, your vertebrae collapses slowly and your internal organs get pushed into slightly different positions towards the front.

Your metabolism also slows significantly so the extra flesh around the waist is not always a sign of over indulgence but nature's way of distributing all your organs.

In Angela's experience, the women who are the closest to another body shape naturally are the ones most likely to change body shape as they get older.

Angela will give you an example here:

Angela's client Tracey's body shape measurements are:

BUST: 93   WAIST: 85   HIPS: 100.5

Tracey's bust is only 7.5 cm smaller than her hips, which lands her in the PEAR shape category. It will depend on Tracey's changes in her body as she gets through menopause to see if her shape will remain in the PEAR shape category or if she moves to RECTANGLE.

It happens regularly that Angela measures women who are on the cusp, so she wanted to make you aware that you could be in the same situation.
When you feel your shape has gone through changes, simply do the measurements again to confirm that you are still working your shape to the max!

Like to Look Fabulous, Taller and Slimmer?

If your answer is YES, then you might be interested in Angela's first book called

8 Ways to Look Fabulous, Taller and Slimmer by Dressing the Best for Your Body Shape.

You will learn incredible tips on how you can instantly look slimmer as well as create a wardrobe you love.

This book is available for Kindle on Amazon. Simply type in the title or search on Angela Barbagallo.

Your Profile

Your profile is the side view of your face. It is a very important characteristic of your face and your hair style can balance your profile perfectly. Penny and Angela will discuss the four main profile types below: Straight, Concave, Convex and Low Forehead/Protruding Head.

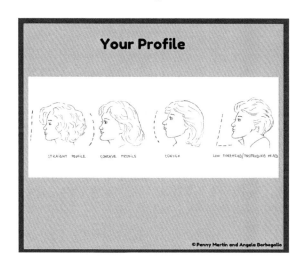

Straight

The straight profile does not have the usual look as the nose is small and the cheeks are protruding, so to pull the hair all back and away from the face may enhance the straight profile.

Using the hair as a dominant feature is a way of pulling the observers attention away from this design flaw, by using a soft waved look or by using colour in the hair can help to draw attention away from this look.

You can also create depth and shape by pulling the sides of this hair design back, but leaving length down at the back and creating fullness on the top to slim the face down.

Concave

This profile will see the forehead and chin stand out and nose area dip in, (looks kind of caved in, in the middle). Because the angles of this look can be sharp and hard, a wavy or curly hairstyle can be used to soften the individual's look.

The hairstyle length that would work well is 2cm below the chin line (or longer) when dried and wavy. This will help to detract away from the over-bite chin.

Usually the teeth sit with the bottom over the top of the top teeth, which makes the chin stick out. Thanks to modern dentistry we tend not to see as much of this in 1st world countries now.

Hairstyles that are pulled back or short hairstyles are not good because they expose the entire jaw.

Convex

This profile will see the chin and forehead recede back and the cheeks and nose become the dominant features. Because this profile angle can make the person look weighty and shapeless in any contouring of the face, then a hairstyle that gives height and lengthens the face can be a benefit.

Taking the hair back at the sides but keeping the length at back can be an advantage as it can make someone look slimmer.

Low Forehead/ Protruding Head

If you have a low forehead it is best to stay away from a short fringe cut because this will box your face in, enhancing the fact that your forehead is relatively smaller.

A longer side sweeping fringe is a great alternative or request the length of your fringe to sit at nose, lip or chin level.

You could also consider wearing your hair back with height as this helps to counteract your protruding jawline as your profile will have a softer balance.

Your Body Size

The ideal is to balance your hair with your weight and look. For example, short hair will not look as flattering if you are overweight.

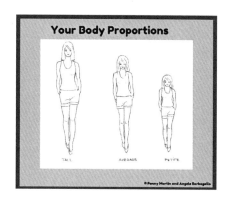

Your Body Proportions

TALL   AVERAGE   PETITE

© Penny Martin and Angela Barbagallo

If you are small in stature and overweight, long hair does not look flattering.

The myth is that short hair is the only way to go when you're older, but there are other flattering options.

Your Ear Size and Protrusion

With big and uneven ears, hair needs to cover the ears and up-styling hairdos need to be loosened in this area.

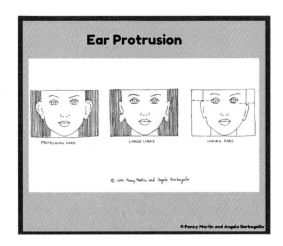

Your Nose Size and Jawline

If you have a large nose, a full, big hair style with height at the crown will help you to minimize the nose.

A square jaw line would suit a short haircut with soft curls or fullness at the crown. A narrow chin would look best with long hair and fullness at chin length.

What is Your Hair Personality?

First impressions take only a split second to form and your hair style and colour are the "big kahuna," the "lead role," of your entire look. It is such an important feature that Penny and Angela would like to dedicate a whole section to connecting you to what your hair style personality is.

Throughout history there have been links to hair and sexuality. Hair effects your psyche. When you love your hairstyle you feel good.

The sexual nature of hair in some cultures insists that it be covered up, or be cut off to symbolize sexual morality, celibacy or punishment.

Over the years redheads were often seen as being promiscuous or in the Middle ages they were called witches.

Blonde hair, being seen as vulnerable, and dark hair seen as being strong and threatening. Long and shiny hair are often seen as being seductive.

Face and body shape are all well and good but, really, it is *YOU, your personality* that reigns supreme on what hair style compliments YOU! You might be lost at this point, and you have no clue to what your hair personality is, so here is a quick fun checklist for you to complete.

Simply tick what is most appropriate and add up the ticks at the bottom.

NATURAL	✔	FEMININE	✔	CREATIVE	✔
you have a no-fuss, comfortable dress style		you love beach-swept, soft and feminine hair		you love looking different	
you want an easy-to-maintain hair style		you love spending time getting ready		you like trendy haircuts	
you like low-maintenance hair colouring		you follow the soft and feminine hair trends		you like bold hair colours and highlights	
you are a sports mum on weekends		you love shopping on the weekends		you love browsing at markets	
you'd rather stay at home or catch up with friends		you enjoy going to a trendy cocktail bar		you enjoy going to music festivals and theaters	
you are conscious on what you spend on your hair		your hair and nails must look great no matter what		you value recycling and the environment	
you live in suburbs suitable for kids and teenagers and sports		you live close enough to a mall for your shopping sessions		you live close to the city and cafés with great coffee	

Your Perfect Hair Style Matches

Now that you have an idea of your hair style personality, let's have some fun in sharing a few great styles and colours Penny and Angela think you will love and that are harmonious with *YOU*.

There is nothing more confidence boosting than YOU feeling great about YOU and, well, let's be honest, your hair is a huge component of this.

Your Hair Characteristics

Genetics are a large contributing factor to your hair type.

Good hair is very much down to genetics. So, if your mum has good hair, so will you.

Your hair doesn't regenerate and what the maximum hair length is is different from person to person.

The cortex is where colour pigments live and all the chemical processes of colouring take place.

Did you know that when you put Asian hair under a microscope it is *round?* Caucasian hair under a microscope is *oval,* and African hair under a microscope is *flat.*

Hair Culture

Each hair culture has specific characteristics that really affect the way your hair is styled and coloured.

There are three ethnic hair cultures: Caucasian, Afro and Oriental. Each group having distinct hair characteristics and the reality of many inter-cultural marriage and subsequent children are showing signs of blending hair characteristics.

Caucasian Hair Culture
Caucasian hair is oval when it is put under a microscope. Caucasian hair also has a large variation in hair colour, from dark to red to blonde.

The average hair shaft diameter measurement shows that 70% Caucasian people have fine hair.

Redheads often have the coarsest hair.

When an association between hair colour and baldness was found it showed that blonder hair has the greatest susceptibility of showing signs of boldness.

Caucasian hair suffers the highest percentage of male hair loss.

Penny and Angela's rating for Caucasian hair:

Afro Hair Culture
Afro hair is flat when it is put under a microscope. Afro hair is usually frizzy and very small in diameter. Afro hair colour is usually black.

Black women have the highest incidence of traction hair loss which means gradual hair loss, caused primarily by pulling force being applied to the hair. This commonly results from the sufferer frequently wearing their hair in a particularly tight ponytail, pigtails, or braids.

Penny recommends that chemical straightening Afro hair every 12 weeks is better then using hot styling and pulling techniques daily. Afro hair is so fragile and vulnerable due to its thinness and twisted configuration which makes it very weak in places along the hair shaft.

Penny and Angela's rating for Afro hair:

Asian Hair Culture

Asian hair is round when it is put under a microscope. Penny always gives her apprentice hairdressers the tip that when they cut Asian hair they put closed-toe shoes on, otherwise this hair can pierce skin like a needle!

Asian hair type is the strongest, with a capacity to grow long often over 40 inches/ 101 cm's. Hair extension and wigs hair are often collected from Chinese, Japanese and Indian hair.

Long Asian hair can be 9 years old, the shedding rate far less, and the incidents of baldness are far less in this hair culture. For the small percentage of women with Asian hair who suffer hair loss, it appears worse due to the dark colour of their hair contrasting with their white scalp.

Penny and Angela's rating for Asian hair:

HAIR TYPE	DESCRIPTION	HOW TO CONTROL
Asian Hair	Straight and slippery.	Use hairspray, or your own choice of styling product, while manipulating the hair. This technique will help to give hair texture and help you control it. Multi-shading techniques of colouring also help to give this hair texture.

HAIR TYPE	DESCRIPTION	HOW TO CONTROL
Thick and dense Caucasian hair	If short, it can look like a wig.	Allow more time. Take one section at a time, work each panel until the style is complete. Multi-colouring the hair also helps it to appear more textured.
Fine Caucasian hair	Sparse fly-away and see-through.	Bulk up with special hair products, use hot rollers, and teasing. Hair pieces and extensions.
Naturally curly Caucasian and Afro hair	If short	Use lots of moisturizers, mousses, and waxes, etc. As above, and do one small section at a time.
	If long	If you're leaving it curly, don't comb or brush it, use your fingers to section it. If straightening, use products before, during, and after, followed by a straightening iron.

Hair Texture

Hair texture is how thick or narrow your hair shaft is in diameter. If you have coarse hair, it will generally be harder to colour than if you have fine hair.

Generally, fine hair tends to be more porous and more easily absorbs atmospheric humidity. You might recognize this if you have fine hair as your hair style goes flat quicker.

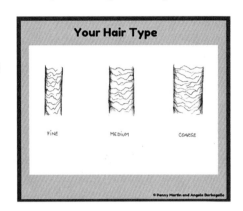

Hair Density

Hair density is how many hairs are on your head. Can you see your scalp easily or is your hair so dense it takes ages to dry. It is like when you're going to buy a good quality rug, and the sales assistant explains the difference in quality of rugs where the pile is so thick and lush that you can't see the backing through the pile.

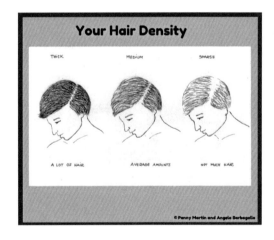

So, do you have a Persian rug?

Hair Growth Patterns

Hair growth pattern can be the cause of potential haircut and styling problems.

Here you will find all the potential hair growth patterns and what you can do about them.

Information is everything, so make sure you discuss your area of concern with your hairdresser.

Hair Growth Pattern	Area on your Head	What can be done
Cowlick - your hair grows up and away from the natural fall position.	At the front hairline.	Keep your fringe weighted to hold the hair down by not layering. Try changing your part to the other side.
Widow's peak - the hairline is a Dracula look-a-like.	At the front hairline.	Avoid styles that pull the hair all back and away from the face. Use highlights to soften the face. Add softness to the hair style.

Hair Growth Pattern	Area on your Head	What can be done
Directional growth pattern	Could be anywhere on the head.	Keeping your hairstyle longer will create more weight to cover this area.
Diffused hair loss	Could be anywhere on the head.	This is a common problem. Possible causes are mainly due to stress, diet, genetics, and hormones. You should seek medical advice.

Facts About Hair Loss for Women

Thinning hair, receding hair line and hair loss often causes lots of distress at any age in a female's life.

Hair thinning in women is just as common as in men but without the extreme form in baldness. Thinning hair for a woman can represent a loss of femininity.

Receding hairline in women otherwise known as *frontal fibrosing alopecia* is a condition where a woman's hair line recedes in some extreme cases for up to 5 inches. It mostly, affects women around the scalp, forming a band like pattern of hair loss.

The average scalp is covered with 100,000 hair follicles. No new follicles are formed after birth. Most people lose between 50-100 hairs a day—but a consistent loss of 150 or more hairs a day is considered a significant hair loss.
Hair loss that is caused by medication, stress, lack of protein or iron, or hair care may be prevented.

Avoiding certain medicines, reducing stress, getting adequate protein and iron in your diet, and having hair styles that don't damage your hair (known in the trade as a chemical hair cut) may reduce or prevent hair loss.

Penny has seen lots of hair loss in her studio over the years. The reasons can vary from client to client and at different stages in a person's life time.

Penny and Angela recommend that you seek medical advice.

Here is a brief overview of the main common causes for female hair loss.

Common Causes of Hair Loss in Women

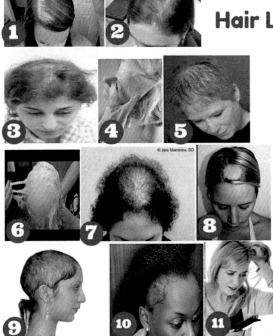

Common Causes of Hair Loss in Women

1. Polycystic Ovarian Syndrome
2. The Pill
3. Pregnancy
4. Menopause
5. Hysterectomy
6. Chemicals in hair colour
7. Androgenetic Alopecia
8. Alopecia Areata
9. Telogen Effluvium
10. Traction Alopecia
11. Gastric Sleeve
12. Hormone Replacement Therapy (HRT)
13. Anemia

Medical Issue	Reason	What to do
1. Polycystic Ovarian Syndrome (PCOS)	An endocrine disorder where women typically have high levels of androgen (male) hormones. Androgen affects the menstrual cycle. Can cause oily hair, acne and facial hair growth. Can occur in young women.	Get a blood test. Get professional advice. Get an ultra sound.
2. The pill	The main hormones used in the pill are Estrogen and Progestin or both and may affect hair growth.	Get a blood test. Get professional advice.
3. Pregnancy	Hair is usually great in pregnancy with increased oil production, however after giving birth 50% of Caucasian woman will experience hair loss.	Get a blood test. Get professional advice.
4. Menopause	Major hormone changes. Can occur before, during or after your body is in full Menopause. The changes almost always affect hair growth resulting in thinning hair.	Get a blood test. Get professional advice. Look after yourself and your diet.

Medical Issue	Reason	What to do
5. Hysterectomy	Hormone imbalance after removal of the womb.	Get a blood test. Get professional advice.
6. Over working your hair by chemicals or Styling Often referred to as a chemical hair cut in the hairdressing trade!	You have yourself to blame for this common issue. Hair can be fragile. Maybe you have used too many chemicals that are found in bleaches and lightening type colouring. Perming. Straightening. Keratin treatments as well as some shampoos. Aggressive brushing, back-combing. Swimming pool water, air pollution and too much UV exposure	Use a protein treatment. Be gentle with your hair. Don't put chemicals on the mid-lengths and ends of your hair. Wait for it to grow back. Look after it!

Medical Issue	Reason	What to do
7. Androgenetic Alopecia	Hormone imbalance where too much male hormone androgen like DHT is present in body. Hereditary factors can be common.	Get a blood test. Get professional advice.
8. Alopecia Areata (areas of baldness in patches)	An inflammatory reaction is behind Alopecia Areata. A person's own immune system attacks the roots of hair follicles. In most cases a stressful situation has occurred which may still have effects on the hair six weeks to three months after the stressful incident. Your body is reacting to stresses that your mind does not recognise.	About 70% of people recover their hair within two years, whether or not they receive treatment. Natural therapies can really help such as relaxation and meditation techniques, yoga, acupuncture.

Medical Issue	Reason	What to do
9. Telogen Effluvium	For some women, Telogen Effluvium is a mysterious chronic disorder and can persist for months or even years without any true understanding of the triggering factors or stressors. Your body's immune system attacks itself.	Nothing can be done. A wig may be an option. Relaxation and meditation techniques, yoga, acupuncture.
10. Traction Alopecia	Trauma to the hair follicles from tight hairstyles that pull at the hair over time including braiding, cornrows, tight ponytails, and extensions.	Stop pulling your hair too tightly. Stop hanging hair extensions onto your hair because your hair clearly can not take the extra weight. The hair follicle may recover and grow back. Use a crayon, spray, eye shadow to minimize shining of the scalp.

Medical Issue	Reason	What to do
11. Gastric Sleeve Surgery	Drastic change in nutrition and eating habits, which is even more pronounced if the patient does not eat the right quantity of nutrients and micronutrients needed during her recovery phase. This may cause some protein deficiency, iron and other minerals like zinc and vitamin B. In addition, weight loss causes hormonal changes that are beneficial for health, nevertheless they are still changes to your body and hair reflects these changes.	If the patient is aware of the type and quality of nutrition to be carried out after the procedure, the chances of losing a considerable amount of hair are very low. Know which high protein foods you can and should eat and which supplements will help prevent hair loss.
12. Hormone Replacement Therapy (HRT)	Ongoing hair loss may be experienced due to androgen (male) hormones.	Hormones need to be restored. Get a blood test. Get professional advice.

Medical Issue	Reason	What to do
13. Anemia	Lack of Iron.	Get a blood test. Get professional advice. Eat protein or take a supplement to build up your iron levels.

Tips and Tricks for Hair Loss for Women

Use a crayon or spray specifically designed to cover the scalp to help minimize the shining of the scalp. If you can't find a crayon or spray, then use eye shadow to darken your scalp and help to disguise the hair loss.

Go to the chemist and purchase Women's REGAINE® Regular Strength Solution. REGAINE® can help reverse the progression of hereditary hair loss in some women. REGAINE® contains minoxidil, an ingredient proven to regrow hair by stimulating hair follicles. Use as directed.

Keep your hair hydrated and trimmed to help strengthen the hair.

Try acupuncture to stimulate hair follicles.

Facts on Hair Loss for Men

You may have a son, husband, brother or father whose confidence is crushed by thinning hair. Please open the conversation and share the chapter below with them. It may be life changing for them.

Generally, hairy men are seen as being more virile. Ancient warriors are often depicted with full beards. You may remember the story of Samson losing his strength when he lost his hair. For some men, hair loss may equate to loss of virility.

It is often difficult to separate the "snake oil" remedies from the genuine solutions because people advocating for or against different products tend to have stakes in the industry too. There is a lot of misinformation out there about what causes hair loss and how it can be prevented.

Here is some hard science to expose the myths and give you the information you need about what you can actually do to keep (or get back) your hair.

In men, hair loss occurs on the front hairline and forehead and on the top of the head. Bald spots are noticeable.

There are several causes of hair loss. However, male-pattern baldness is the most common type of hair loss and is typically permanent. It accounts for about ninety-five percent of hair loss in men.

Male-pattern baldness is a condition that can be inherited from either the mother's or the father's side.

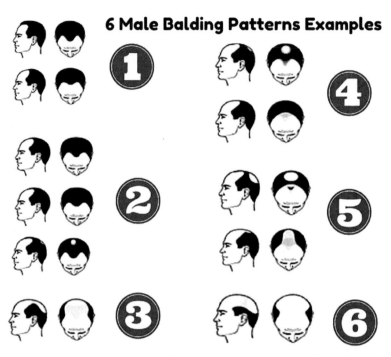

6 Male Balding Patterns Examples

Male-pattern baldness can start in your teens, twenties, or thirties.

Male-pattern baldness affects up to one-third of all men.

By the age of 50, approximately fifty percent of men have significantly thinning hair.

Hormones play a big part in hair loss for men

It's not normal to lose 150 or more hairs a day.

It is a complete myth that baldness is inherited from only the mother's side of the family. You hair future is determined by genes from both sides of your family and you have likely ended up with some mix of your parents' hair genes.

Overworking your hair can damage hair, making it weak and easily broken. Processes that may cause hair troubles can include aggressive brushing, back combing, straightening, and dyeing. Chemicals in shampoos, water, air pollution, and too much UV exposure can weaken the outside and inside of hair fibres.

Stress can be a factor in hair loss problems for example, after something drastic like a car crash or the death of someone close. Otherwise, stress is not likely the cause.

However some hair loss problems have proven to be a mystery even to some of the professionals. It seems as unique individuals, our immune system can cause some hair loss problems as the body can sometimes attack itself. Penny and Angela highly recommend consulting a dermatologist with a referral from your GP. The dermatologist will diagnose the condition and recommend appropriate treatment. They may even refer the patient to a hair transplant professional. The hair transplant professional may do the individual grafts of transplanting the hair from your nape area to the areas that have been affected with hair loss and transplant your own hairs from one place on your head to the other. This is called Follicular Unit Transplantation which has proven to be a successful technique.

Follicular Unit Transplantation (FUT) is a hair restoration technique where a patient's hair is transplanted in naturally occurring groups of 1 to 4 hairs, called Follicular units. Follicular units also contain sebaceous (oil) glands, nerves, a small muscle, and occasional fine vellus hairs. In Follicular Unit Transplantation these small units allow the surgeon to safely transplant thousands of grafts in a single session, which maximizes the cosmetic impact of the procedure.

FUT is considered an advance over older hair implantation procedures that used larger grafts and often produced an unnatural look. In a properly-performed follicular unit transplant, the results will mimic the way hair grows in nature and will be undetectable as a hair transplant.

Penny and Angela's compassionate advice is to act whilst your son or husband is young and/or still has hair. Should they have a predisposition to hair loss then try and keep their hair follicle alive and act sooner than later. This will save them a lot of money too as this surgery is very expensive...ask famous cricketer Shane Warne who is the poster child for hair loss!

It is a total myth that wearing baseball caps too much will cause you to lose your hair. Your baseball cap would have to be on your scalp so tightly that you couldn't wear it in order for it to cause any type of traction or damage. In other words, your cap would have to be pulling hair out of your head (a lot) in order for it to cause permanent hair loss.

Tips and Tricks for Hair Loss for Men

✓   Go to the chemist and purchase REGAINE®. REGAINE® is the first available clinically proven treatment for hereditary hair loss in Australia. It helps reverse the progression of hereditary hair loss and, with revolutionary Men's REGAINE® Foam (the only proven hair regrowth foam), REGAINE® continues to lead the way in topical products for regrowing hair. In clinical testing, nine out of ten men kept or regrew their hair after they used REGAINE® Foam twice daily over sixteen weeks. REGAINE® Foam is quick and easy to apply, plus it dries in no time at all, so it will fit easily into your daily routine. Use as directed.

✓ Keep your hair hydrated and trimmed to help strengthen the hair.

✓ Try acupuncture to stimulate hair follicles.

Cancer Treatments and Drug Side Effects that Cause Hair Loss

Hair loss can be a side effect of many drugs. Always read the manufacturer's instructions, read the information leaflet provided, always ask the chemist and of course your doctor.

The most common is Chemotherapy when treating cancer.

Hair loss is a common side effect of chemotherapy treatment for cancer.

Hair loss due to chemotherapy unfortunately cannot be avoided. Penny and Angela's advice at this sensitive time is to focus on returning to full health with the support of good friends and health professionals.

A "Look Good Feel Better" program exists in Australia where hair and makeup artists assist with wigs and makeup application to enhance self-esteem and help cancer patients through the treatment journey and back to health. Penny has on numerous occasions been asked to go to people's homes and cut their hair off prior to chemotherapy. A hair cutting ceremony is held with a group of supportive friends. The hair is cut off instead of letting it fall out as a result of the chemotherapy as the stress of the hair coming out in handfuls can be even more traumatic. The hair is cut very short, not shaved or clipped, as this is too traumatic, then Penny shows them how to fit and style a wig or scarf.

A beautiful box is prepared to store the hair and end the ceremony.

When the hair grows back it may seem to have a different texture or is curly but often just goes back to what it was before the chemotherapy.

Chapter 4
Hair Colour

It is needless to say that if the walls of Penny's salon in Arncliffe could talk, they would be able to fill a few volumes of terrible hair disasters that have been fixed by Penny.

Let's start at the beginning.

As a hairdresser, managing timed appointments is an important part of managing a successful salon and providing good customer service. Having an idea on what type of service she needs to provide on a particular day—for example, a total revamp; or a colour correction; or just a maintenance type of appointment—enables Penny to determine the time required to provide the service.

The points which are important when Penny analyses for colour are the following:
- ✓ Previous colour
- ✓ What colour you would like
- ✓ How to achieve your desired colour and its maintenance

Basic consultations involve three questions:
- ✓ What do we have?
- ✓ What do we want?
- ✓ How do we get there?

Hair colouring can be extremely technical; it is not as simple as just choosing an eye shadow and painting it on. The questions above are paramount to the success of the target colour. Some colours just *cannot* be done and may need a longer term plan to achieve them. Timing for these services can vary from one and a half hours to eight hours!!

An experienced hairdresser is more likely to be honest with you and not under deliver your expectations.

For example, a client that has had black dye in her long hair for numerous years, and now wants to go pale light cool blonde, will be dreaming to think this will happen after one application. This, in fact, may realistically take six months.

If a client, who is naturally very dark, wants to go to a pale white blonde, it may be better for her to wear a wig than to subject her poor hair to the endless bleach applications and the maintenance program of keeping the image looking like that.

Many clients want the balayage look and then realize their hair has become extremely dry and brittle. This is due to the chemical compounds used, so it's very important to use good products that fill the shaft with proteins and moisturizers to hydrate the hair.

It is important to think of the long-term effects on the hair shaft and if your hair can take these harsh chemical changes.

Are you "of a sound mind" in making a radical hair change, or are you "having a moment"?

You may like to ease yourself into a change by having a good treatment and a blow dry. Yes, there is always more to hair than just hair, and it is always good to have a thorough consultation so you're happy with your decision.

One good thing is that your hair will continue to grow, so it's great to have fun with styles and colours while you can.

Your Colour History

If you have never coloured your hair, this is called a *colour virgin*. With virgin colour hair, any colour direction is easy for a hairdresser or a supermarket home colour to achieve the colour you desire.

But the reality is that not many of us are a colour virgin AND you may even have dabbled in some home colour experiments.

This means that your hair shaft is filled with existing artificial dyes, and your hairdresser is in colour correction mode.

It is important to know, as your desired colour choice might take about six months to be realistically achieved without any tears.

It's like a painting a wall—the preparation is so important.

Your Colour Choice

To help your hairdresser to achieve your desired hair colour, it would help to have a mood board with a collection of hair colours you love.
Upon making your hair appointment, find out the level of colour skill of the hairdresser. A hairdresser needs to be incredibly skillful in order to mix and apply the right amount of chemicals to your hair to achieve what you desire without completely destroying your hair.

For example, describing *"blonde"* to a hairdresser means at least five different levels of blonde and two different tones of blonde—warm or cool.

Showing the hairdresser a sample of your favorite shade of blonde will get you talking the same language and it will leave interpretation out of it.

At the beginning of your appointment, you should not only get clear on the shade but also if your hair will be able to take it. There are lots of chemicals involved in colour changes!

Colour Basics 101

Knowledge is power, so here are some basics that all hairdressers should know. And, having some colour facts up your sleeve might help you to be one hundred percent confident that your hairdresser is experienced enough to give you the best results.

Basically, if they don't know what you're talking about when you mention the information below, you may like to ask for the Salon Manager or race out of the door!

This is an overview to explain to you in simple yet technical hair dressing language how, for example, your hair might turn green when you go from light to dark; or how your hair may look flat/matte/lifeless when you go from blonde to dark; or, when you have gone from dark to blonde, why it looks orange or yellow.

It's like a science lab.

Here we go ...

Describing Hair Colour

The hair colour we see consists of depth and tone. Hair also has an undercoat of colour, called undertones, which only come into play when we lighten or colour the hair.

Universal Number System
There is a universal number system in hairdressing.

The first number denotes the *colour depth*. Depth refers to how light or dark the base colour of the hair is. It is sometimes called *level*, with dark hair having a low level and light hair having a high level. It doesn't take into consideration variations in colour, just whether your hair is very dark, very light or somewhere in between.

In hairdressing terms, there are 10 depths: black, darkest brown, dark brown, medium brown, light brown, dark blonde, medium blonde, light blonde, very light blonde and lightest blonde.

All are neutral shades. The higher the number from 1-10, the lighter the shade. For example, 1 is black and 10 is the lightest blonde.

Depth/Level (Base)

10.0   Lightest blonde/pale
9.0   Very light blonde
8.0   Light blonde
7.0   Medium blonde
6.0   Dark blonde
5.0   Light brown
4.0   Medium brown
3.0   Dark brown
2.0   Darkest brown
1.0   Black

Natural redheads will usually be somewhere between levels 3 (dark auburn) and level 7 (strawberry blonde).

This level system is somewhat up to interpretation so one person's light brown is another's dark blonde.

You may also see 12 as the first number on a hair colour (on Wella hair dyes, for example) and it usually indicates a high-lift, ultra-light blonde shade. It's not a natural depth level.

Tone/Reflect

The second number denotes the *tone of colour*, from *warm to cool*; it is also called *reflect*.

Warm tones have reds, yellow and orange in them, and are in colours such as strawberry blonde, copper and chestnut brown.

Neutral tones have a balance of warm and cool pigments in them.Cool tones have blues and greens in them, and are often referred to as ash tones.

For hair colouring products, the tonal quality of the finished result is often given as part of the colour description (e.g. intense red, honey blonde, rich copper, light beige blonde, deep chocolate).

So for example, when you walk into a salon and you have a colour in mind you would like to achieve then this will be achieved by the level of base shade and the reflect that you desire.

Reflects are based on primary colours. Now, this might freak you out a little, but these are the colours:

WARM: YELLOW, ORANGE, and RED

COOL: GREEN, BLUE, and PURPLE

Below is the hair dressing lingo for these primary colours:

Colour Tones/Reflects

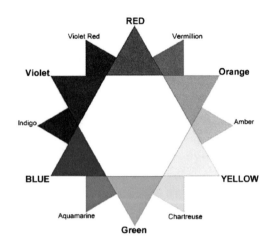

Yellow = blonde
Orange = copper
Red = red
Green = matt
Blue = ash
Purple = violet

Now you know the difference between depth and tone you can work out what colour you can expect based on a hair dye's numbering system.

Let's take the example; L'Oreal Diacolour Richesse in 6.23 "Mocha Gold". 6 is the depth of colour. Referring back to the

depth chart above you'll see that 6 is a dark blonde. The part after the decimal point refers to the tone.
Unfortunately manufacturers tend to number the tone differently. This system is known as the International Colour Chart (ICC) but there's nothing standardised about it.

Let's take a look at L'Oreal's numbering system.
Natural – 0
Blue Ash – 1
Violet – 2
Gold – 3
Copper – 4
Mahogany – 5
Red – 6
Green Ash – 7

So 6.23 is dark blonde with a dominant tone of violet (2) and a secondary tone of gold (3). It makes quite cool-toned colour.

Some manufacturers will use letters instead of numbers such as Goldwell:
N – Natural
A – Ash
BV – Blue Violet
V – Violet
R – Red
B – Brown
G – Gold
K – Copper

RB – Red Brown
The letters here can also denote intensity; a 5RR would be more vibrant than a colour labelled 5R. You can see that

based on this lettering system the L'Oreal 6.23 would translate to 6VG although you can expect a bit of colour variation from one manufacturer to the next.

So if that all seemed a bit confusing it's because every manufacturer numbers (or letters) their shades slightly differently and the only part that's universal is the depth number. Typically hair stylists will train in one brand and learn their numbering system.

Undertones

Your natural hair has an underlying warm tone, dictated by the amount of the pigment *melanin* found in your hair.

There are two types of natural pigment: *eu*melanin and *pheo*melanin.

Natural Pigment: Eumelanin vs. Pheomelanin

If you have light or red hair it will contain predominantly pheomelanin. Pheomelanin is a yellow to red pigment. The lighter your hair the less pheomelanin it contains. Some hair has a mixture producing our unique natural hair colour.

If you have black to brown hair it will contain predominantly eumelanin. Eumelanin is a black to brown pigment.

The undertone becomes more evident when hydrogen peroxide is used to lighten the hair. It also shows through when hair is naturally lightened from exposure to the elements like the sun.

Melanin is slowly oxidised during colouring and can produce those difficult-to-remove golden and orange tones in the hair. Undertone can affect the final colour result when dyeing hair. When dark hair is bleached sufficiently, it will go from having a red tinge to orange, yellow and, finally, white as the melanin breaks down.

As we now know, underlying pigments are the natural pigments that make up every hair colour. When formulating hair colour, they must take into consideration the underlying pigments and how they will act on your hair.

Your hairdresser will need to determine if the underlying pigment will help or hurt your desired outcome. If you are looking to achieve a cool beige blonde on natural level 6 hair, then, in this case, you would lose the underlying pigment and work to cover up the warmth that will inevitably come out in the hair when you lighten it.

Keep in mind that you'll generally have to be aware of underlying pigment when you are lightening two shades or more from the natural hair colour level. You won't have to worry about it when going darker than the natural level.

Going Lighter Underlying Pigments

With the process of going lighter when having to use bleach (especially when trying to lift artificial colour) as you pull up the pigments—like tiles being pulled up from an old floor—it will start to expose underlying pigments as seen in the table below.

Counteracting Colour Pigments

These counteracting colour pigments are used to fix and neutralize the unwanted colour pigments. It does this by counteracting the reflect that you don't want to see. It's very clever!

From Blonde to Dark Fillers

Well, as the lessons of life go, whatever you steal you must put back. So, fillers are used to put back the underlying reflect of the desired level and shade you are intending to go to.

How are fillers mixed and applied? Fillers are mixed with warm water, placed sparingly of top of the light blonde bleached sections of your hair, then allowed to dry. Then, we mix and place your target shade level of colour over the top!

Level of base shades universal numbering system in hair dressing	Going lighter underlying pigment	Counteracting colour pigments	From blonde to dark pigment fillers
10 - Lightest blond	pale yellow	violet	diluted yellow
9 - Very Light blond	yellow	violet	yellow
8 - Light blonde	yellow	violet	yellow
7 - Medium blonde	yellow/copper	violet/blue	yellow/copper
6 - Dark blonde	copper	blue	copper
5 - Light brown	copper	blue	copper
4 - Medium brown	copper/red	blue/green	copper/red
3 - Dark brown	red	green	red
2 - Very dark brown	red	green	red
1 - Black	red	green	red

Let's Get Practical With Base Shades and Reflects

What the reflects are used for is to give, for example, a warm caramel shade in a highlight, or a cool ash in a base colour, or to add some warmth to black hair.

Warm Caramel Beige: level 8.0 Light Blonde with yellow and a touch of green (go figure ---> green...!!) will give your hair a beautiful highlight.

Cool Ash: Level 6.0 Dark Blonde with blue will give an ideal colour for middle-aged ladies.

Warm Black: To give warmth to black, you would add red to a level 1.0 Black.

Cool Black: To cool black hair, you would add level 1.0 with blue.

Using Base Shades and Reflects to Change Your Colour

From Dark to Blonde
Two things need to happen. Firstly, the hairdresser needs to look at your existing hair colour (with virgin hair there is no need for this). Secondly, depending on the level of blonde you would like to become—from level 6.0 let's say upwards to 10.0—they need to take the *existing* colour out of your hair.

Depending on the existing colour, and more importantly, the condition of your hair right now, a goal plan to achieve this desired colour may be best spread over a twelve month period to ensure the hair shaft can handle the strain.

From a level 1 black to go to a level 10 blonde is simply impossible if you want to keep the hair on your head. However, you could make a plan to lift level 1.0 to level 6.0 and then from level 6.0 to level 9.0 or 10.0 over twelve months.

Make a plan. You could go shorter! Often, you will see bleached-white blondes with very short hair styles, like the singer Pink, because of the damage it could cause.

You could also go multi shades of blonde by using foil packages and making it a lighter blonde in-between. This saves your hair from the stress, and you still look primarily blonde!

Blonde to Dark
If you are naturally blonde without any colour in your hair (what is called virgin colour), OR if you are blonde through existing hair colour, and you want to go dark, first decide which level of dark you would like to be. Have a look at the correlated reflectors in the table above.

A simple example: let's say you're a level 10.0 blonde and you want to be a level 6.0 blonde, then your hairdresser would fill your hair with yellow with a touch of orange.

Whatever has been stolen from your colour, the pigments will make it look vibrant and make you look younger. If you don't add the pigments, your hair will look unhealthy, matte, and flat, and you will simply look ill.

Bleach, Colour and Peroxide

Penny and Angela have noticed a lot of confusion about what it means to use bleach versus colour or peroxide in your hair. This book would not be complete without sharing the most important differences between these three hair colour components. You will be armed with knowledge next time you have your hair done.

Bleach

Bleach is a powder, it is used to remove the colour pigments from the hair shaft. Bleach is strong and can damage your hair if the incorrect dosage is used. For bleach to remove the colour pigments, it must be mixed with an "activator" called hydrogen peroxide for the chemical process to work.

Colour

Colour is like paint and comes in a metal tube, it contains colour pigments, and many other ingredients to help open up the hair shaft to deposit colour. There are numerous different colours and shades. Colour must also be mixed with hydrogen peroxide to activate and make it work. The peroxide strengths used are 10 volume and 20 volume which deposit colour into your hair shaft. The other two strengths are 30 volume or 40 volume are used to highlight your hair shaft.

Peroxide

Peroxide also called hydrogen peroxide or H_2O_2, is like water but with an extra oxygen atom. The oxygen is used to oxidise the colour and make it work. The oxygen is also used to activate bleach and make that work Peroxide come in various strengths: 10 volume, 20 volume, 30 volume and 40 volume, with 10 volume being weaker than 20 and so on. 10 and 20 volume peroxide is safe to use on the scalp. However 30 volume and 40 volume have restraints: they can only be used on very dark hair, for highlights away from the scalp or for mixing with high-lift specialised colours.

The packet mixer in the home colour kits packet mixer only ever have a strength of 10 or 20 volume to prevent serious accidents.

Using anything stronger than 30 volume when mixed with bleach and applied directly on your scalp could cause severe burns and would cause your hair to snap off. This is called a "chemical haircut".

A mixture of bleach and peroxide can lighter hair irrespective of what colour has already been on your hair previously.

A mixture of colour and peroxide can only lighten virgin hair that has not been previously coloured with an artificial darker colour.

Coupons and "Fantastic Deals"

The trends using coupons to get a "fantastic deal" might not only cost you more money in the end, they might lead to months of damage control.

Let's look at this: *why would a salon need to sell below-cost hair deals?* They would only consider it if they didn't have enough clients. They go fishing and "give" away the vouchers so you would, hopefully, come back in the future.

Once you have paid for the service, the salon could easily lose interest in making sure that they give you excellent service and a fantastic hairdo. You get what you pay for!!! Don't be fooled by the "great deal" as YOU have to walk around with the results on full display for six months.

Horror Colour Stories

A lady had a bad experience with her very moody male hairdresser who had a go at her. The result was so bad, and the client was so upset, she decided to buy a home-colour kit. (Her hair is super fine, very curly, and very dry.) It turned khaki green! She booked in Penny had to use a colour stripper to get the pigment out.

Here's a another story to send shivers down your spine ...

Penny remembers a client being left alone as colleague hairdresser in the salon forgot all about her!

The hairdresser had numerous clients underway at the same time and had used bleach, glad-wrap, and put the client under a drier to speed up the chemical process. *Note to your hairdresser: they should never use a hair dryer when bleaching.*

Penny remembers looking over, realizing what was happening, grabbing the client, running to the basin, rinsing the client's hair, and watching as her hair washed down the drain!!! This is called a *Chemical hair cut*, no charge! Poor hairdresser— over worked and under paid!

Bleach is not to be messed with, once you reach pale yellow/white the next stop is drop off!

Practical Tips for "Grey" Hair

There is no such thing as a grey hair. It is, in fact, a white hair that looks grey against the other darker-coloured hair and is devoid of any natural colour pigment.

You MUST look for moisture adding products like a "leave-in treatment" product. Your hair will be dryer because of the white hair and possibly existing hair colour.

To cover the white hair Penny recommends never choose a fashion colour. A natural base shade must be added to make up for the fact that no pigments exists in the hair shaft of your white hair. The only effective way to colour your hair is to use a permanent colour instead of a semi-permanent colour. Semi-permanent colour would just not be strong enough to cover your white hair.

Your white hair loses moisture content and will become coarser and a bit wiry, or it could present itself as more textured.

As you age, your complexion will lose colour too, and your eyes will become smaller and duller.

Tips for Ageing Hair When You Have Dark Hair
Consider going a bit lighter and maybe using multi shading to blend the white hairs coming through. Soften and pretty it up a little. Use foils around the hairline and the top of the hair;

the back can stay your own colour. After a full head of colour, you may like to do a regrowth maintenance.

Tips for Ageing Hair When You Have Red Hair

Your hair is cooling, it will become more strawberry blonde, and it will change colours. Penny and Angela suggest that you put more red streaks back in or, alternatively, ask your hairdresser to go lighter and put warm blonde foils in. If you decide to go with a full head colour then the regrowth line will be a huge upkeep so plan your colour for easy maintenance!

Tips for Ageing Hair When You Have Light Hair

You are in a lucky position because your white hair will largely go unnoticed. You may want to keep your foils up to blend in your white hairs.

Home Colour Kits

Did you know that per capita Australians use more hair colour than anywhere in the world!

Your budget and time may be stretched, and sometimes using a home colour kit from the supermarket is the way you choose to maintain your look. Your dollar can only be spent once.

The reality is that many, many women use the do-it-yourself home colour kits, and this chapter educates you beyond what the package tells you, so you are armed with the right information.

Here are some of Penny's tips, techniques, and "what to do" in case of a disaster so you end up with hair in the right shade, without it snapping off or looking green or orange.

But, lovely lady, Penny and Angela do not take any responsibility, as they truly believe that you need a qualified colour technician who knows what they're doing.

Before you go any further, always protect your bathroom and yourself from dye stains. While you want to stain your hair, you do not want weird blotches of cherry red all over your sink and favorite clothes.

Cover any surface around you that might get dye on it and put a sheet or newspaper on the floor. Have paper towels nearby to deal with spills. Wear an old top you don't like, preferably one you're ready to throw away. It is very easy to get dye on what you're wearing, just compare it to the cape you wear in a salon.

Coat your hairline, ears, and neck before applying dye to your hair. You can use Vaseline, lip balm, or the conditioner included in the kit (if one is provided). Applying this coating will make it easier to rinse off the dye that gets on your skin.

Permanent Home Colour Tips for Blondes

If you are a lovely shade of blonde and you put any semi-permanent colour in your hair that, according to the packet, washes out in about six washes, you might be surprised. As, gorgeous lady, this is not the case. Be aware that it will not wash out completely because it has stained your entire hair shaft.

You could compare it to washing a white sheet with a black sheet. It never goes white again, and it has a grey colour. There are two ways to get it out: use a colour stripper or bleach.

Age of Your Hair

When you use a home colour it is not only the colour, the application is just as important because your hair is a natural fibre.

Your hair will absorb colour like a sponge. The older your hair, the more porous it is. For example, long hair is maybe three years older than your roots. Plus, new hair is like virgin hair and not filled with leftover colour from a previous colour session. The longer and older hair at the bottom will suck up the colour faster than in the newer hair bits.

Active Ingredient in Colour

Once bleach (which is not a colour) or ANY hair colour has been mixed and the chemical reaction has taken place, the ingredients will be active for one hour ONLY. So you will not need to leave the bleach on for longer than that. It will not make your hair lighter.

Bleach must be mixed with an activator to enable it to work. It is usually mixed 1 scoop to 35 ml of peroxide. However, you can cheat with the measuring and just look for a good consistency like a cake mix, not too hard and not too soft.

Hair colour is usually stored in an airtight metal tube. It is usually mixed in equal parts with the activator peroxide.

The mixed colour is now ready to be applied to the hair shaft and, at this stage, the molecules are still small and can be squeezed into the hair shaft. As the process evolves, the oxidized colour pigment becomes bigger and gets trapped in the hair shaft, so it can no longer get out. This is now your new beautiful hair colour!

All colours contain the colour pigments called para-phenylenediamine (para dye for short). The darker the shade, the more para-phenylenediamine it contains, even the herbal tint that you purchased from your health food store. This is what can cause severe allergic reactions and sensitivities which will be covered in the next few pages.

What Is Ammonia?

Ammonia is used to help open up the hair shaft to allow chemical processes to go inside, passing through the cuticle layer to the Cortex layer where all hairdressing treatments are done.

There is a global push to remove ammonia from hair colour over the next few years to make all hair colour ammonia free.

Here are some insights to the components of your hair.

Your hair shaft has three layers:

1. **The Cuticle** looks like fish scales that are overlapping. Hair that is in great condition and looks very shiny has lots of overlapping well-conditioned cuticles.
2. **The Cortex** is the layer hairdressers love, as this is the layer they use for all their chemical processes. The cortex makes up the bulk of the hair; this is where all the colour pigments live, both natural and artificial. Ammonia has a distinct smell (like wee!) and there is a global push to remove ammonia from all colour tints. Ammonia-free hair colour can be found in chemists' and salon only based tints. When all is said and done, you are using chemicals on your scalp, so minimize exposure, and take good care of yourself in all the processes.
3. **The Medulla** is in the middle (like the lead in a pencil). Hairdressers don't need this layer and not all human hairs actually have one.

A Note on Herbal Tints

Natural herbal tints are in fashion but they still need to be used with the same level of caution as you are still dealing with chemicals. The difference is that herbal tints have no ammonia, which is used to open up the first layer of the hair shaft. Herbal tints have been formulated with some other chemicals, like peroxide. The beauty industry is working towards all colours being ammonia free.

Test for Allergies

The box may look pretty and the (famous) model on the hair colour box may look gorgeous, but you are about to handle serious chemicals that can potentially be a health risk for you.

Before you apply the colour, read the box, and you will see the recommendation to test this colour solution on your skin for allergies twenty-four hours prior to applying it to your scalp. Please do not ignore the allergy warnings!

This is all because of the chemical para-phenylenediamine (para dye for short). The darker the colour, the more of this chemical is used, and the more likely you are to be allergic to this shade.

The allergic reaction could make your airways swell up. So, they recommend HIGHLY that, when you're about to colour your hair, you follow these simple rules:

1. Test for allergies - ALWAYS!
2. Have someone in the house who knows you're colouring your hair and who knows what to do in case of an emergency allergic reaction.
3. Put rubber gloves on!!

Quantity of Product

If your hair is long and dense (so lots of it) you may need to buy two packets to cover your hair in your desired colour. You don't want to be caught running out of a product halfway through the application.

Comb Web-Sectioning Technique

This ***comb web-sectioning technique*** is *crucial* when you're using a home colour kit to maintain your colour.

Instead of putting all the colour on top of your hair, you need to section your hair with the sharp end of your comb in small 8 mm sections from the front to the back, almost like a spider web. You apply the colour to the middle of the section to the left and the right covering your regrowth.

This is a tricky technique but crucial for great results. You will find a detailed video to the Pinterest Hair and Face Shape Board on how Penny uses this ***comb web-sectioning technique*** to get the best results at home! Simply search for styleangel3 on Pinterest.

Covering Regrowth and Grey Hair

If you want to remain the same colour and you are just covering the regrowth or grey hairs, then use the comb web-sectioning technique. It allows you to put the colour directly on the roots and regrowth ONLY, so you are not damaging the middle to ends of your hair as they will go darker as that part of your hair is much older and has been filled with colour lots of times, compared to your newly grown virgin hair. If your middle to ends need refreshing, then add water to dilute any colour left in the bowl and apply to the middle ends to ends for the last five minutes of the total processing time.

For Dramatic Colour Change

From Blonde to Dark Hair
Choose a brown that is WARM (and has gold or copper already premixed in the colour) and practice the comb web-sectioning technique.

Apply product to all the regrowth first and wait twenty minutes for processing, then put some water in the bowl to dilute the solution.

Add a little watered-down product to your scalp to wet the remains of your hairs (please note: don't use too much or it will wash out!) and emulsify the colour all the way to the middles and ends of your hair. Your hair should now have colour all over it.

Forget the processing time on the box. Use your eyes and watch your hair go darker. As soon as it has reached your desired shade, wash it off because the middle to ends of your hair are porous and old and will grab the colour so fast that it could speed out of control and go much darker than it showed on the box.

Ideally, use a shampoo and conditioner with a pH value of 6.5 because it stops the action of colouring chemicals in its tracks. You will be able to find your shampoo's pH value via your internet search engine. Repeat the regrowth maintenance as per above.

Dark to Blonde
If you have virgin colour hair, read the instructions on the box, and you'll be fine. Please note that the darker your hair

is, the more orange the outcome could be. The blonder your natural colour is, the more true to the colour on the box you will end up with. Good luck!

If you have any existing artificial colour in your hair, then colouring your dark hair blonde is probably going to turn into a nightmare. Penny and Angela really recommend that you go to a salon and pay the money.

If you have light brown hair, and you want to go a few shades lighter, you must choose a bleach solution and not a box of colour because it won't take. Colour over artificial colour will go darker.

Hairdressers learn this at school. You have to use bleach. When applying bleach, everyone's hair will react differently. The lighter your hair, the less time it will take; the darker your hair, the longer it will take.

Apply the bleach 2 cm away from your scalp and, because of the heat coming from your scalp (this is called the heat band), the colour will go lighter much more quickly. Apply from mid-ends to end, wait fifteen minutes, then immediately apply it to the roots with the comb web technique for the remainder of the processing time. However, keep your eye on the shade. If you see the desired colour, then wash it off using the shampoo with a pH balance of 6.5 and a conditioner.

You must use a toner that can come as a semi-permanent colour or a temporary colour in the form of a mousse or lotion. It will have a violet look when it is mixed because violet counteracts the gold that is left in your hair.

This colouring process can be explained as follows: when you go from dark to light, inside the hair shaft a little fight is going on. In pulling out the colour pigments and bleaching them, you're often left with an unwanted reflect/overtone. This could be red, orange, or yellow.

The toner is used to counteract the unwanted reflects. It may not say the word "toner" on the box. However, a colour level of 9 or 10 with an ash reflect will do this. On wet, shampooed, and towel-dried hair, do the comb web-sectioning technique very quickly, keeping away from the hairline, as the hair is finer, and the ends, as the hair is more porous.

Use your eyes to see if the yellow is being counteracted by this colour. When you see that it is the desired colour, put your head over the sink or in the shower and emulsify by rubbing the ends of your hair all together so the toner is now on your ends and hairline as well. As soon as you have done this, shampoo and condition it all thoroughly. Rinse your scalp really well.

As an example, if you leave the toner on your ends and hairline too long, it could possibly turn into a lovely shade of violet or blue!

The packaging will not usually mention any problems or the techniques widely used by hairdressers. This is why the packaging has a help line because many women have huge problems with this. Be prepared if your hair is very dark—you could end up with orange hair, and you may need two boxes of bleach on the same day.

The fashion colours are red, orange, yellow, green, blue, and purple (and, hopefully, not all together at once!) This may not be for your own hair. You may have a rebellious teenager at home playing with hair colour kits, so you may be able to help them get the right shade they want and get some brownie points as a cool mum.

Unless you are a very light natural white blonde, then you need to pre-bleach because you need to get your hair shaft to a pale blonde before you can apply any of these fashion colours to achieve these true bright fashion colours. Please follow the steps for full head bleaching. There is no need to use toner. Instead, put the fashion shade on and leave it on for the full processing time stated on the box.

Frequently Asked Colour Troubleshooting Questions When Bleaching Your Hair

Hair Too Red
If the hair is too red, buy another box and repeat the process. Make sure you master the comb web technique. Repeat the process until you hit yellow.

Hair Too Orange
If the hair is too orange, buy another box and repeat the process including the toner. Repeat the process until you hit yellow.

Hair Too Yellow
ONLY repeat the toning process straight away.

Hair Too Violet/Blue

This happens because your hair is porous and there are different ages of your hair. This is not necessarily stated on the box. Colouring your hair is a very unpredictable process with lots of risks, and you need to be confident to apply the techniques given to you in the chapters above. Penny and Angela recommend that you are actively involved in the processing time and not just rely on the box.

Hair Too Green

This happens possibly due to colouring your hair from blonde to dark and just putting the packet dark mix straight on without pre filling your hair with the correct underlining pigments. If the underlining pigments are not returned then your hair can go green and look very flat.

Artificial blonde hair will need to be filled, remember what you originally "stole" from the hair will need to be put back. If you want your hair to go back to black or very dark brown, then the underlining pigment is red.

If you want your hair to go back to a mid brown, then the underling pigment that you need to fill your hair with is orange (copper).

Let's say you are an artificial blonde who wants to go lighter blonde (a level 8 blonde or more) then yellow must be returned.

The other possible situation for green coloured hair is when blonde haired children have been swimming in a heavy chlorinated pool and the chlorine has reacted to give a green reflect.

Here are a few ways that can be used to fix this
1. Use a clarifying shampoo and do a high cleanse shampoo. A high cleanse shampoo is designed to remove toxin-related metabolites from the hair shaft. You are able to find high cleanse shampoos by doing an internet search.
2. Do a bleach wash by mixing bleach with peroxide, warm water and a bit of shampoo. Apply on the green strands of hair only. Rinse this solution out thoroughly and follow by your normal shampoo and conditioner.
3. Try tomato sauce, the acid pulls out the green and the red is opposite to green on the colour chart and will counteract the green!

You Have Over-Toned the Hair
To get rid of this, buy another box of bleach, mix it up as per the instructions, put gloves on, and add 10 ml of warm water and 5 ml of shampoo. First, shampoo, condition, and towel dry your hair so it's still wet. Second, stand in front of a mirror and apply the bleach to the violet/blue sections only.

This should take between one to ten minutes maximum, but keep watching the shade until you reach your desired colour. As soon as the unwanted overtone is gone, shampoo as usual. If it is patchy, then shampoo it all off and just put the remainder of the solution on the remaining violet/blue sections and wash your hair again thoroughly. To avoid this in the future, keep your eye on the toner and don't rely on the processing time on the box.

Hair Snapped Off
(In the trade, this is known as a Chemical Haircut)
This is a messy situation, but you may be able to salvage some parts of your hair that have not yet broken off by purchasing a protein conditioner and leave-in moisturizers.

This will really help to mend and glue together the hair shaft that is breaking apart. It's a bit like poly-filler on a wall.

Why has this happened? Your hair is made out of keratin (a protein) which is a natural fibre that dies when it comes out of your hair follicle in your scalp. As with any natural fibre, there is only so much it can take. If you trash a silk shirt by throwing it in the wash with jeans, it won't last.

The ends of your hair can be very old and need to be handled with care. The coarser your hair, the more likely you are to get away with mistreating your hair with home care products. The finer your hair, the more fragile it is, and it really needs to be treated with care by you and your hairdresser.

Your Scalp Has Blisters
Shampoo and rinse everything off thoroughly even if it stings and apply full-fat cream milk from your fridge directly onto your scalp and all over your head. Leave it for five minutes and then rinse it off. Please give your hair and scalp a chance to recover, which will take about three days.

Yellow Overtone Maintenance
Using a blonde shampoo which is a shampoo with a violet/ blue colour molecule which is designed to counter balance gold. It neutralizes yellow overtones to help your hair appear

more blonde or white. It's a bit like a laundry soaker that you put in your wash when you're washing whites.

Should I Wash My Hair the Day Before I Colour My Hair?

Wash your hair 24 to 48 hours before dyeing it. This allows the natural oils in your hair to develop, which in turn allows the dye to bind to your hair more easily.

The dye will blend more naturally with your hair and tends to last longer. If possible, avoid conditioner when you wash your hair the day before dyeing it. Conditioner eliminates your natural oils, which you need for the dye to set in more easily.

However, if your hair is extremely dry, condition your hair every day with a leave-in conditioner, to help hydrate the hair shaft and to even out the hair shaft's porosity, ready for the dying process.

A Final Note on Home Colour Kits from Penny and Angela

Penny and Angela don't want to sound like old grandmothers, but *please* test for allergies, and please tell your kids who use these home colour kits to test for allergies.

Be careful while using bright reds or black - they can stain bathtubs.

Choose an old, dark towel, as you will get stains!

If you're using high-fashion colours like reds, coppers, and blacks, please put a towel over your bedding as it may run for the first few washes.

Right now, you might be ready for a nice cup of herbal tea to calm your nerves after reading this colour segment.

Unveiling the processes of home colour kits can be confronting, especially if the marketing around it all looks so pretty, but just know the tresses of those gorgeous models are handled by experts only and the models certainly don't use the home care kits themselves to get ready for their photo shoot.

Information is everything! As long as you're ready for the risks and you know what to do, then a home care kit is a great solution for you. If you are a little scared, book in with a professional! You deserve this pampering and your hair deserves the best treatment available.

Chapter 5

Hair Care

You may have wondered if there is a benefit to buying salon professional products, usually at a much higher price, over supermarket brands. Liken it to a sponge cake versus a Christmas cake—they are both cakes but the ingredients are hugely different.

Shampoo is a cleanser and removes oil, dirt, and product build-up. Conditioners smooth down the outside layer of your hair shaft (cuticle). And, finally, treatments improve the middle layer of the hair shaft (cortex) which makes up the bulk of your hair. All of the chemical services take place in the cortex making this a very important layer to nurture.

Shampoo and Conditioner for Your Hair

Problem	Reason	What to do	Choosing what to use
Oily roots and scalp	Your oil gland is secreting too much oil possibly due to hormones.	Wash your hair daily with a gentle shampoo or a clarifying high cleanser for very oily hair. Put the shampoo directly on the hair without using water first (oil and water do not mix) then apply the shampoo. The molecule in shampoo disperse the oil. Rinse with plenty of fairly hot water. Do not put conditioner on the scalp only use conditioner on the ends of your hair.	pH shampoo. Clarifying Shampoo. A very light conditioner. Many brands have clarifying shampoo ranges and light conditioners to help with this problem.

Problem	Reason	What to do	Choosing what to use
Oily roots and scalp but dry hair	Your oil gland is secreting too much oil possibly due to hormones. Dry on the mid-length and ends of the hair due to either age of the hair or chemicals.	Wash your hair daily with a gentle shampoo or a clarifying high cleanser for very oily hair. Put the shampoo directly on the hair without using water first (oil and water do not mix) then apply the shampoo. The molecule in shampoo disperse the oil. Rinse with plenty of fairly hot water. Do not put conditioner on the scalp only use conditioner on the ends of your hair.	pH shampoo. Clarifying Shampoo. A very light conditioner. Many brands have clarifying shampoo ranges and light conditioners to help with this problem. Conditioner for dry hair on the ends only. Time saving Tip: In-between shampoos, just zone out the front part of your hair and just shampoo that part.

Problem	Reason	What to do	Choosing what to use
Dry roots & scalp	Lack of natural oils which usually occurs in the winter season.	Choose a moisturizing shampoo and conditioner with hydrating qualities.	Many brands have hydrating/ moisturizing ranges to help with this problem.
Coloured/ chemically treated	From colouring hair with all kinds of hair colour products.	Handle your hair with care. You will need need moisture balancing products. Some ranges actually have the colour pigment added into the products.	Many brands have colour treatment ranges to help with this problem. Choose colour pigment matches: - Blonde choose purple reflect to help with yellow tone of the hair. - Red heads choose red-pigmented products to keep the red module fresh.

Problem	Reason	What to do	Choosing what to use
Fine/ straight Flat/ limp	From the hair being fine in diameter Sometimes this hair type also gets oily quickly.	Needs volumising a chemical service, like colouring bleaching, perming can help by swelling the hair shaft, increasing the diameter and helping your hair to look thicker. Lies flat, looses its style quickly is to heavy and gets over loaded quickly.	Many brands have volumising range to help with this problem. The shampoo and conditioner needs to be light and not too heavy or it will overload the hair and make your hair look flat.
Curly/ frizzy	Natural curly also could be naturally Afro type of hair	Need moisturising, lots of shine spray and leave-in conditioner. They contain oils and silicones. Be aware they can create build up which can attract dirt and then it can look dull again.	Many brands have moisturizing ranges to help with this problem. Moroccan oils products are great for this hair type.

Problem	Reason	What to do	Choosing what to use
Dandruff	Scalp flaking. (Big flakes) Real name Pityriasis capitis simplex for dry dandruff. Pityriasis steatoides for oily dandruff. Mainly found in people with an oily skin. The skin naturally sheds, but when there is a higher intensity of shedding and mixed with your natural oil secretion it creates big flakes you know as dandruff.	Metabolic changes. You can help improve dandruff by reducing your stress and eating healthy foods. Penny and Angela recommend to get a hormone blood test.	Many brands have medicated or anti-dandruff ranges to help with this problem. The chemist often have Sulphur based or Coal-tar based products than can help with dandruff.

Problem	Reason	What to do	Choosing what to use
Dry sensitive (flaky) scalps	Flaking scalp. Often confused with dandruff.

To make it worse the treatment for dandruff will really aggravate this condition.

The skin naturally sheds, however the skin is very sensitive, dry and often tender. | The scalp needs lots of moisturising and needs to be handled with care. | Goldwell has a sensitive range

Many brands have hydrating/ moisturizing ranges to help with this problem.

Not many brands have a sensitive range. |

The ingredients in professional products are more expensive to manufacture than the supermarket brands. Most supermarket brands are full of *non-water-based silicone* products. These types of cheap silicones are a hairdresser's worst nightmare, as they react with most of their chemical products, particularly colour.

Hairdressers agree that supermarkets make the products smell great, just so you are enticed to keep using the products, but the *danger* of using these lower cost hair products from the supermarket for your hair, your health, and the success of your future colour jobs is high.

When a reputable hairdresser recommends their hair care products to you, it's not just to improve the bottom line of their business. It's to help with the compatibility of the hair service procedures undertaken and to improve the condition of your hair.

Facts about Silicones

A common misconception about silicone-based hair products is that silicones are bad for your hair.

The fact of the matter is that silicone products themselves are not bad for the hair.

Instead of being concerned with silicone ingredients, you should be concerned with the TYPE of silicone agents in your hair products.

There are two types of silicones: **water soluble and non water soluble silicones.** Water soluble silicones are ones that can be washed away with water and nothing more. Non Water Soluble Silicones cannot be washed away with just water.

Non Water Soluble Silicones require the help of sulfate shampoos and conditioners in order to remove the silicone coating from the hair. If you're trying to retain moisture, then you may want to refrain from using non-soluble silicone products such as sulfates that strip the hair of its natural oils.

Although water-soluble silicones only require water to dissolve them, water-soluble silicones may still be bad for the hair.

If you have a hair routine that requires daily moisturizing, then water-soluble silicones may not be a good fit for your hair either, unless you *co-wash* frequently.

What is Co-Washing?

Co-washing is short for "conditioner washing," or cleansing your hair with your favorite conditioner instead of shampoo.

Textured hair has a natural tendency to be drier than straighter hair types. The natural oils created by the scalp have a harder time navigating the twists and turns of curly hair. All conditioners have a small amount of gentle cleansers and those conditioners can and should be used more than shampoo to clean curly hair.

Co-washing is becoming so popular that hair product companies are offering co-washing cleansing conditioners along with gentle sulfate-free shampoos.

Depending on your hair and other factors, such as your schedule and the climate, you can co-wash as frequently as you like.

Keep in mind that your hair is the most fragile when it's wet. Be careful in styling, and allow your hair time to dry completely before washing again. There is such a thing as over-conditioning, so pay attention to your hair's feel. If it's spongy or even mushy, you're overdoing it.

Wash Occasionally With a Sulfate-Free Shampoo

As with any type of silicone, either water soluble or non-soluble, the coating on the hair prevents moisture, protein, or other products from penetrating the hair shaft.

Additionally, when an overload of silicone products are applied to your hair, the buildup from the silicone coating eventually causes breakage. That is why it is important to **wash** your hair after using silicone products to prevent buildup.

Your hair and scalp still need adequate cleansing with a gentle shampoo. When you skip the shampoo for too long, your scalp might become itchy. Shampooing weekly or bi-weekly in addition to regular co-washing is recommended.

Co-Washing Is Not For Everyone

If you suffer from scalp conditions such as dermatitis, co-washing occasionally is okay. But a strict co-wash regimen could make this condition worse. Also, depending on your hair type, you may not see the benefit of co-washing. If you have oily hair, a shampoo is needed to remove excess oil, as a co-wash can add extra oil to the hair.

Silicone Selection

As a general rule of thumb, if you want to know if your hair products contain silicone agents, just read the label.

Look for products that have "cone" as an extension. For example, dimethicone is a silicone because of its "cone" extension.

Water Soluble Silicones
Dimethicone copolyol
Lauryl methicone copolyol
Hydrolyzed wheat protein (hydroxypropyl polysiloxane)
Any silicone with PEG as a prefix

Non Water Soluble Silicones
Trimethylsilylamodimetheicone
Dimethicone
Phenyl trimethicone
Cetearyl methicone
Dimethiconol
Amodimethicon
Stearyl dimethicone
Cyclomethicone
Cetyl dimethicone
Cyclopentasiloxane
Behenoxy dimethicone
Stearoxy dimethicone

Expert Guide to Styling Products

There are endless styling products on the market so Penny and Angela have put together a guide to what products you need to achieve your look as well as how and when to use them.

PRODUCT	BEFORE STYLING	DURING STYLING	AFTER STYLING
Leave-in treatments	For very dry and damaged hair, leave-in treatments help to resurrect the hair shaft to a healthy looking state.		
Straightening balms	Help to control and relax frizzy curly hair (note they can get smoky while blow-drying, so don't worry).		
Setting lotions	Used for roller setting, assists in keeping the style in for longer.		

PRODUCT	BEFORE STYLING	DURING STYLING	AFTER STYLING
Water spray (use a fine mist)		When static is in the atmosphere (dry windy days) or over-drying the hair.	
Dry shampoo (talcum powder)	Use on the roots to dry up oiliness when you don't have time to wash the hair.		
Straightening balms	Help to control and relax frizzy curly hair (n.b., they can get smoky while blow-drying, so don't worry).		
Coloured hairsprays			Can make the hair look textured or just for fun, photo shoots, runways. It is an instant wash-out hair colour.

PRODUCT	BEFORE STYLING	DURING STYLING	AFTER STYLING
Hair thickeners	Great for Caucasian, fine hair as they work by encasing the individual strand, plumping them and making them appear thicker. Some products also use a magnetic charge to repel each strand of hair against the other.		
Wax			On dry hair only (not wet) [oil and water do not mix] Leaves hair oily and healthy looking, can help to define a curl—be careful at the roots as it can look greasy

PRODUCT	BEFORE STYLING	DURING STYLING	AFTER STYLING
Pomade	Can leave hair wet looking and shiny.		Can leave hair looking shiny and healthy.
Thermal	On dry hair, on each section, as you put in a hot roller or straightening iron, this will help protect the hair from the heat.		
Smoothing complexes/ shine serum Sheen sprays			On the ends to mid-lengths Makes the hair appear healthy and calms down those shorter fly-away pieces.
Gel	Can leave hair wet looking Can be dried in to help hold a style.		

PRODUCT	BEFORE STYLING	DURING STYLING	AFTER STYLING
Mousse	On wet hair before styling to define a curl.		Great on naturally curly hair to help give curl a definition.
Hairspray	On dry hair, e.g., with hot rollers To help control slippery hair (Asian) Spray on the roots to dry-up oily hair.	While styling	To set the design for a longer lasting finish Helps protect against weather conditions Helps to smooth down the short, fly away hairs.

The Science of Blow-Drying

Your hair will stretch sixty percent when it's wet and twenty percent when it's dry. Hair is a fantastic medium to work with, as it will allow you to re-form it in different shapes.

There are two ways of achieving these shapes. You can either style from *wet hair* to *dry hair* by using a hair dryer or hood dryer, or from *hot* to *cool hair* by using hot tongs, hot rollers, or straightening or crimping irons like a GHD.

The best thing about it is that when you change your mind, as most women do, you can re-form it into a different style, as this sort of styling is only temporary, not permanent.

Blow-drying can make curly hair wavy or straight hair curly by breaking the temporary bonds by stretching the hair around a brush and then drying it with a hair dryer.

When you blow-dry your hair and you have lots of it, then start at the front and work towards the bottom as you might get tired after a while. Go back to your fringe and go over that again at the end. Blow-drying in sections is also a great help to get the job done fast.

If you're after more volume in your hair, then try the following movement. Take a medium amount of hair strands and roll them around your hairbrush. Instead of just blow-drying the strand, position your dryer underneath your hair so you literally lift from the roots. You will like the effect of this instantly.

If you are after straighter hair, then always position your hair dryer facing down and away from your roots to the end of your hair.

Tips on Brushes

✓ Pure bore bristle brush
✓ No metal comb (only good for dog hair)
✓ No plastic brush as it will cause static hair

✓ Metal in the inside of the brush will help with molding shapes and heats up hair like a hot iron

✓ No slippery handles

And of course check the back of your hair in the mirror when you're finished, as everyone looks at you from the back.

Our Expert Opinion on Keratin

What is Keratin and What's Happening With Keratin?

Keratin was seen as a revolution in de-frizzing and smoothing the many textures of hair from curly to relaxed.

The naturally recognized training in Australia adapted and put keratin in the new training packages to train apprentices, and it was here to stay as part of the repertoire of services available to the general public.

However, the buzz about the treatments was not all good, mainly because many of the brands on the market contained formaldehyde. Formaldehyde can be toxic, allergenic, and carcinogenic.

Ironically, the government did not pick up on the levels used until many complaints had been received from salon workers and customers who had inhaled the formaldehyde fumes.

This is another case of technology advancing faster than government legislation. The product came with government legislation of a material safety data sheet (MSD). However, formaldehyde is converted from liquid to gas as it is dried into the hair shaft and then ironed in to lock it in place.

Formaldehyde is also used in nail polish and in embalming fluid.

What adverse effects does formaldehyde have on humans?
- ✓ It is responsible for causing headaches and burning sensations in the throat, which can trigger asthma symptoms in some people.
- ✓ It is classified as a carcinogenic.

Most, if not all companies' products, were recalled off the shelves and reformulated to an acceptable level.

It's also interesting to note that the large cosmetic companies, like Goldwell, did not put a keratin treatment onto the market *at that time*. These companies are very reputable and never want a class action lawsuit in the future. However, Goldwell has just released a product that combines keratin and silk molecules, with zero percent formaldehyde, which Penny now uses in her salon.

Only smaller boutique keratin manufacturers brought keratin treatments into the marketplace originally. Those boutique keratin manufacturers are now non-existent, quite possibly due to the backlash of harmful and dangerous ingredients.

So, are keratins safe? The treatments have evolved so much over the years on the market. Customers no longer complain about the smell. However, a chemical is needed to make the process work. And to get shiny, straight hair for months, formaldehyde or other aldehydes must be used.

Thank goodness Australia has an acceptable level for human use in place with the workplace safety legislation (as opposed to America, for example).

As Penny and Angela mentioned, Goldwell has just released a keratin product into the market place, which combines keratin and a silk molecule. From Penny's experience, it is great and leaves your hair looking shiny. However, it will not give you three months of straight hair as the original ones did. But, the absolute positive compromise is that this Goldwell keratin product is much safer for you and the hair dressing industry.

Bottom line, the choice is yours when it comes to deciding if these treatments are right for you.

About The Authors

Thank You

Penny and Angela are blessed with amazing clients like YOU, and they are deeply grateful you have taken the time to read their work of passion!

Please reach out to us if you have any questions!

About Penny Martin

Penny Martin has a passion for hair! She creates hair designs with exceptional creativity and durability so you have GREAT hair! That's what she's here for.

Hair Stylist, Penny Martin

She has the BEST job in the world! On a daily basis, she gets to help women like you look great.

She also provides a personalized, enjoyable experience ensuring you look and feel amazing.

Penny has built a reputation as the most experienced, reliable, and respected bridal and hair design specialist in Sydney.

People say Penny is a miracle worker with hair. She can do anyone's hair and make them look their best including really 'hard to do' hair.

Penny has over thirty years of experience doing hair plus fifteen years teaching other hairdressers at TAFE and private colleges.

Hair is her passion, and she keeps up to date with the latest fashion trends and technological advances in hair styling.

Penny has had the pleasure of working with clients from Australia, Italy, Greece, Canada, America, UK, Hong Kong, India, and China.

Penny also has a passion of advocating for underprivileged groups, such as Youth at Risk, intellectual disabilities, and juvenile justice for girls.

Penny has worked in rehab facilities with a colleague calling themselves "the fun team" motivating and inspiring people. Penny has also been a student counselor.

Penny believes in a fair go for all and is a great believer in second chance opportunities, as no human being is ever perfect.

Penny considers herself lucky that she really likes people!

About Angela Barbagallo

Angela Barbagallo is one of the brightest minds in personal styling and confidence coaching today.

For over fourteen years, she has contributed to the increased confidence of thousands of clients in how they feel about themselves. She has educated them into making great style choices, which translates into increased feelings of well-being and a positive attitude in life.

Personal Stylist,
Angela Barbagallo

Her guidance to many men and women on how to dress in the corporate world and how to ensure that the way you dress matches your capabilities, has no doubt contributed to her clients' successful career paths, confident return to the workforce transitions for many women, and increased promotional chances.

She has formal qualifications in Colour and Body Shape Image Consulting as well as a Bachelor of Hotel Administration of the prestigious hotel school The Hague, in The Netherlands. Angela's background in five-star hotels working for Hyatt in the early '90s now translates in giving each client an outstanding experience either in a group or as an individual.

Angela was appointed NSW Stylist for Diana Ferrari in 2011 as part of their Fusion Reward Program. Angela also collaborates with the Swiss ultra-premium skin care and makeup company, Arbonne, which allows her to offer a complete make-over service by providing expert skin and makeup advice to her clients.

In providing her clients with as many confidence tools as possible, Angela has launched her first Amazon book in her Confidence series with the title *8 Ways to Look Fabulous, Taller and Slimmer by Dressing the Best for Your Body Shape.*

Angela's life purpose is to give people and teams confidence in how they look. People's confidence will lead to the world being a more beautiful place and that is exactly the spark that started Style Angel many years ago in a time when hiring personal stylists was not the "in-thing".

Client Reviews

"Liam and I would like to thank you so, so much for helping me look so fab on our big day. You were professional, warm, and creative through the entire process. Your guidance was more than appreciated, and I will treasure the look you created for me for the rest of my life. I have never, or will never, feel so beautiful and glamorous again in my life. Thank you so very, very much."
Cassandra

***

"You helped make my wedding day absolutely amazing, not only doing all those whose hair I had booked, but somehow managing to do the three extra I had forgotten about. Your bubbly personality guaranteed a great start to our day, and I am happy to say I am no longer *hairdresser phobic*. You have totally restored my faith in hairdressers (and miracles)."
Jen

***

"After knowing you as a friend and my hairdresser for over fifteen years, I know what a true professional and great hairdresser you are, but you still surprised me on my wedding day. I have always trusted your judgment and you have never let me down. I truly thank you for having the ability to read my mind and produce exactly what I envisaged. Many, many thanks."
Louise

***

"Thank you so much for the wonderful job you did with my hair on my wedding day. I absolutely loved it; it was perfect. Everybody commented on how lovely it looked and asked who

had done it! I still can't believe how you can transform hair like that. It is a real talent that you have and you are a true professional. It was the best day of our lives. Thank you for all of your help. You are a lovely person and a true gem."
Nicola

***

"How could I begin to thank you for all you've done for me? Without you, I know I would never have made it to the church. I can't begin to tell you how much I appreciated the beautiful job you did on my hair. It was pure perfection and exactly what I pictured (how did you know?). But I have to thank you from the bottom of my heart for being there when I needed you most. You're a very special person, Penny, and I feel extremely privileged to have been able to meet and spend time with you. All the very best to you."
Trish

***

"Just wanted to say how much I enjoyed our last couple of styling sessions.

To be able to purchase with confidence both clothes and now shoes and accessories makes shopping a treat, as well as a breeze. You truly are a one-stop shop and 'go to' girl. You have made me feel more confident in my dress and style, you bring with you your beautiful self with so much enthusiasm, love and generosity of spirit. Thank you seems inadequate."
Kerry

***

"With my wardrobe, I always felt like there were some gems in there but were lost among a whole lot of clothes that do not fit or do not suit or were on sale and still have tags on. I was really looking forward to getting some direction about what to shop for, colours that suited me, and to put an end to me buying items that look great on the hanger but unflattering on me.

The whole shopping experience was fantastic. I could see the difference that wearing the right colours for my fair skin tone was making to my overall appearance.

We also found a pair of Mavi jeans that made me lose two kilos instantly! I went home with four dresses, sandals, jeans, a work blouse and trousers, tank tops, and some great accessories, all without breaking the bank.

People comment every time I wear an item we bought together. I could not be happier!"

Barbara

***

"I really enjoyed the shopping experience with you. It was great to learn about colours in particular, and I have been enjoying my purchases.

I think the session built confidence in my ability to determine what clothes suit me well. The black dress is something I am really looking forward to wearing when it gets a little warmer."

Philippa

***

"It was a great day. Angela was very knowledgeable, but not pushy. She knew which shops were having sales (which helped the budget go further) and really got the choice of clothes correct for my style."
Brenda

***

"It was two hours of enjoying clothes shopping. I felt comfortable trying different styles and there was no pressure from Angela. Angela gave me a positive and fresh approach to selecting clothes. I was very sorry when the two hours were gone. I would recommend my stylist with a gold star. Put it on your bucket list!"
Catherine

***

"Well, let me just say, as much as I dislike shopping, I did have a great day. I learned a lot and, as of today, I am absolutely stoked. I am wearing my new sandals (and, yes, my feet don't look as tiny in these). Okay, I may have a pair of Lorna Jane pants on, but I have the watermelon-coloured top from Jacqui E and have had sooooo many people comment on how I look, and they love the colour on me!! Whoo hoo! I'm feeling like I am six feet tall today. I can't thank you enough."

Jennie

***

"I loved the style consultation on Saturday afternoon. On Sunday, I made a real effort to wear soft summer colours and, when I was out shopping in David Jones Tuggerah, a sales assistant came up to me and complimented me on my colour choice in clothes!!!! I told her I had had a consultation the day before."
Fiona

***

Make a HAIR Booking with Penny

Hair - Cutting - Colour - Bridal - Special Occasion

Penny Martin

Salon Address:9 Bellevue St, Arncliffe
Australia

Hair Stylist, Penny Martin

Email: penny@pennymartinhair.com

Website: www.pennymartinhair.com

Call: 0411 122 519

Make a STYLE Booking with Angela

Wardrobe - Personal Shopping - Colour Analysis - Skin Care
and Makeup

Angela Barbagallo
Email: styleangel@me.com

Website: www.styleangel.com

Call: 0407 032 531

Personal Stylist,
Angela Barbagallo

Purchase Angela Barbagallo's
latest Book *8 Ways to Look
Fabulous, Taller and Slimmer by Dressing the Best for Your
Body Shape* on Amazon.

Made in United States
North Haven, CT
21 March 2023